CAMBRIDGE SCIENCE EDUCATION SERIES

Series editor Richard Ingle

The Personal Response To Science

John Head

The right of the
University of Cambridge
to print and sell
all manner of books
was granted by
Henry VIII in 1534.
The University has printed
and published continuously
since 1584.

D0185465

CAMBRIDGE UNIVERSITY PRESS

Cambridge

London   New York   New Rochelle

Melbourne   Sydney

To T.J.G.

Published by the Press Syndicate of the University of Cambridge
The Pitt Building, Trumpington Street, Cambridge CB2 1RP
32 East 57th Street, New York, NY 10022, USA
10 Stamford Road, Oakleigh, Melbourne 3166, Australia

First published 1985

Printed in Great Britain at the University Press, Cambridge

Library of Congress catalogue card number: 84–9576

British Library cataloguing in publication data
Head, John O.
The personal response to science.——
(Cambridge science education series)
1. Science——Study and teaching
I. Title
507'.1   Q181
ISBN 0 521 27808 2

GD

CONTENTS

The author

John Head lectures at the Chelsea College Centre for Science and Mathematics Education, the University of London. Formerly, he taught science in British and United States schools and lectured at St. Paul's College, Cheltenham. In recent years he has worked principally as a psychologist. He was a team leader of the Science Teacher Education Project, a contributor to the Nuffield O level chemistry scheme, an editor of the Nuffield Science 13–16 scheme and is currently a member of the Consultative Committee concerned with the revision of Combined Science. In the past decade he has visited over a dozen countries in four continents as a guest lecturer.

The series editor

Richard Ingle is Lecturer in Science Education at the University of London Institute of Education. He graduated in the physical sciences at Durham University and then taught science in secondary schools for a period of fourteen years in Scotland, England and Uganda. He subsequently held posts in chemical education at Makerere University College, Uganda, and at the Centre for Science Education, Chelsea College, University of London. During the 1970s he undertook an evaluation of Nuffield Chemistry and subsequently became general editor of the revised Nuffield Chemistry series. He was for a time education adviser at the Ministry of Overseas Development. His current interests include the pre-service and in-service education of science teachers, cultural aspects of science education, and probing the difficulties faced by pupils in using mathematics in the course of their science education.

Cover design by Andrew Bonnett

Photograph by Sally and Richard Greenhill

FOREWORD

There is widespread agreement that our school science education is in need of reappraisal. John Head's experience in curriculum development has led him to reflect on the changes of the last twenty years, and this book is the product of a good deal of thought, discussion and research.

Science educators must have a clear view of the nature of science. Science used to be seen as impersonal, and was studied as objective knowledge rather than as a contingent and provisional stage in the struggle for understanding. Research into the learning of science, which focussed on the problems of mastering its concepts, tended to reinforce this view. Scientists and science educators are now committed to a different view, in which both the personal work of scientists and affective elements in learning are seen as important. This book shows that the relation between science education and the social context of beliefs and practices concerning science is closer than generally recognised. The interaction sketched here between adolescent development, the strange logistics of a curriculum which sets up crucial choices for children at ages 13 and 14, and the biases in ideology and the personality of scientists is fascinating in its intricacy and profound in its consequences.

One target for science education is to provide all citizens with a worthwhile insight into the nature and effects of science. Another must be to attract more highly able students to science and technology. These aims are not in conflict and their pursuit requires that we broaden the scope of science education to work more fruitfully with other areas of the curriculum. It is to the credit of John Head's breadth of vision that this optimistic message should have emerged so clearly.

This book is addressed to all those concerned with the development of school science. It provides a secure base for developments now under active consideration and important lessons for the scientific community in how they see themselves, and how they may wish to be seen.

P.J. Black; Director, Centre for Science and Mathematics Education, Chelsea College, University of London, 1984

PREFACE

Even at the beginning of my professional career as a school teacher in Britain and the United States, I felt that science education needed reform and I became actively involved in curriculum development. Although the materials produced by the curriculum projects were intellectually exciting, I still found that many thoughtful students were alienated by what they saw as the cold, instrumental quality of science. The obvious solution was to try to humanise science by stressing its applied and social significance, but attempts to do this have met with caution and even hostility. It has often been argued that science is value-free and objective, and that any discussion of its applications and social relevance corrupts its purity. I was struck not only by this curiously naive view of science, but also by the strong emotions used in expressing it.

This experience caused me to look to psychology for an explanation which would link subject choice to concomitant attitudes and beliefs. Initially, I assumed that the relevant psychology was somewhere in the literature, and that the problem was simply to locate it, but as time went by I realised that clarification could only come from detailed empirical work. The award of a two-year Research Fellowship in Psychology by the Social Science Research Council allowed me to start this work.

My thanks are due to many colleagues and students. I must thank, too, those school pupils and their teachers who put up with the disruption caused by my presence while gathering data. The Director of the Chelsea College Centre for Science and Mathematics Education, Professor Paul Black, has taken a keen interest in the work and has kindly contributed the foreword to this book. For several years Dr Michael Shayer occupied an adjacent office and acted as a penetrating yet kindly critic of my developing ideas. I am grateful to Dr Clive Sutton of Leicester University and to Dr Edward Black of the London School of Economics and Political Science for reading the first draft of this book and making many useful suggestions for improvement. It has been a pleasure to work with so helpful and thorough an editor as Dr Richard Ingle.

John O. Head; Chelsea 1984

1

Towards a Psychology of Science

The literature about science is vast and my justification for adding to it is to offer a different perspective to that usually met. In studies of the history, philosophy and sociology of science the emphasis is either on the impersonal nature of scientific knowledge or on the behaviour of the community of scientists; in either event the role of the individual is played down as being trivial or distracting. This book has been written in the belief that the individual's psychology may be more important than commonly recognised and in an attempt to provide a coherent description of the various ways personal factors may manifest themselves.

Public Knowledge and Personal Understanding

We need to make a clear distinction between what Ziman calls the *public knowledge* of science[1] and the individual's personal understanding. Public knowledge is that contained in the textbooks, or discussed at conferences, and is clearly important as the science being utilised in our society. This aspect of science concerns the historian and sociologist in describing the development of ideas and practices. In such studies stress is laid on the objective, open aspect of science so personal beliefs and values are treated as peripheral idiosyncracies.

Despite this emphasis on the public aspect, science is conceived, understood and propagated by individual persons whose understanding cannot be divorced from the totality of their beliefs and knowledge. An individual's personal understanding is much less than the corpus of public knowledge and it displays qualitative differences. Individuals are selective in those parts of the public knowledge to which they have access. Each person has an incomplete understanding which is incomplete in different ways.

1

Furthermore, personal understanding may involve holding beliefs and explanatory models which are not acceptable as public knowledge, that is to the majority of professional scientists in the contemporary culture. 'The trouble with most folks', runs the old saying, 'is not their ignorance, but knowing what isn't so'.

There are several reasons for being interested in the nature of personal understandings, rather than public knowledge, particularly in education where our concern is with changes in personal understanding. If we listen to a science lesson we might initially examine the general transaction taking place between teacher and class. That transaction is the public knowledge aspect and in those terms the fact that one pupil is looking out of the window, apparently ignoring the lesson, is just a peripheral detail. Yet to that pupil the happenings seen through the window are the focus of attention and the general transaction in the classroom is peripheral, a background murmur of noise. Any science learnt by the pupil at that time will come from events seen through the window, not from the teacher's talk. If we are interested in attitudes to science, and images held of it and scientists, then it is the realm of personal understanding which is under discussion. Other issues – the lack of women involved in science, the concern with the responsibility of scientists for environmental damage, the lack of communication between the 'two cultures' of science and the humanities – might be better understood if the role of personal understandings were appreciated.

Although such a case can be made for paying attention to these personal understandings, this perspective is commonly neglected in studies about science. Not only have historians and philosophers emphasised, or even gloried in the impersonal element, but biographies of scientists have tended to tell us what the scientists did rather than who they were, though the latter can shed light on the former. There are exceptions, but it is noteworthy, to take one example, that most of the participants in Watson's account of the discovery of the DNA double helix structure[2] were opposed to him publishing such a subjective account which described so fully their own foibles. Watson confirmed in his book the suspicion that underlying the well-rehearsed debates about the public knowledge of science lurks the fascinating, but largely untold, story of personal beliefs and commitments, and that reactions of members of the scientific community to new ideas are not merely a product of cool, analytical, objective scrutiny.

The Myth of Objectivity and the Nature of Science

The belief in the objectivity of scientists runs deep. It occurs in the stereotypical popular image of the obsessive recluse withdrawing from personal relationships and all commitments outside science to devote his undivided attention to work. The inductive model of scientific enquiry, with the scientist employing a neutral and unbiased eye to take note of all events, and then solely on the basis of these observations, without prior belief or commitment, generating hypotheses to be subjected to impartial scrutiny by experiments, is still sometimes used in science education, e.g. in *Fable: A Lost Child Keeping Warm* in the ChemStudy textbook[3]. The survival of this belief, certainly in a simplistic form, is remarkable, for it has been challenged by scientists[4], it conflicts with evidence about the nature of perception and cognition, and it ignores the influence of the social organisation of science.

The inductive model starts with the scientist noting all possible observations with an unprejudiced eye and then seeking regularities and patterns. But the psychology of perception tells us that people are highly selective in what they notice, and inevitably attempt to interpret their observations in terms of a prior knowledge of the world. The selectivity factor may well be a protection against perceptual overload. At any instant we are receiving information from all our sense organs, yet we only take notice of one or two of these at a time. While concentrating on a visual image we tend to ignore sounds, while listening to sounds we ignore the information input from the skin and muscles unless the chair is proving too uncomfortable, and so forth. Many current theories of memory postulate the existence of a short-term sensory store in which all these sensory inputs are held for a second or so before either being utilised by the higher brain regions, or being discarded. Certainly selection takes place. Different people walking down the same street at the same time may well take note of different objects, the appearance of the sky, the articles in the shop windows, the faces of the passers-by, and so on, according to their own interests and needs. If preoccupied by thought on a pressing issue the individual may scarcely take note of the surroundings at all and the sensory input is solely used to avoid colliding with other persons.

We cannot avoid exercising this selectivity. Laboratory experiments reveal that attempts to handle too many sensory inputs causes confusion and distress in a subject. The scientist cannot therefore notice everything; a choice has to be made, if only at an unconscious level, to pay attention to particular concerns and ignore others.

It is equally true that we cannot avoid interpreting sensory input in the light of our prior beliefs. Most cognitive psychologists believe that our memories and ideas are not held as separate, randomly scattered units in our mind but are organised into some form of cognitive structure. How new information is received will depend on the form of the existing structure. If the input is coherent and compatible with what already exists, integration should be easy. On the other hand if it is not coherent then a major structural reorganisation is necessary or the new input will be retained as a meaningless form of words, as in rote learning. From early childhood we use our congnitive structure to help us interpret sensory inputs and make sense of the world.

It is easy to see the power of this anticipatory and interpretive function when it in fact yields the 'wrong' answer, e.g. with optical illusions. Illusions depend on appeal to prior knowledge so we interpret the image in the light of previous experience rather than just note what is actually shown to us. The well known Muller–Lyer illusion, as shown in Fig. 1.1, where the direction of the arrowheads diverts our attention from the length of the lines seems to arise from an automatic compensation for perspective displayed by people brought up in an environment containing a large number of parallel lines and rectangular shapes (roads, railways, buildings, rooms, furniture). It has not been found with people brought up in other environments, for example Zulus.

We continue to make interpretations of visual images even when we are aware of the problems that they can produce. Fig. 1.2 shows 'an impossible figure'. As an abstract, two-dimensional design it is unremarkable. Only when we see it as representing something in three dimensions does the problem arise that the figure is

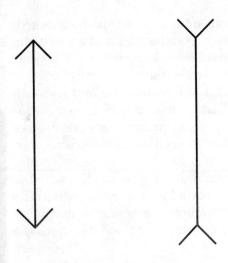

Fig. 1.1 The Muller-Lyer illusion

Fig. 1.2 An impossible figure

not consistent, yet despite that knowledge we still tend to interpret it in three dimensions.

Parallel situations can be found in the 'schoolboy howlers' where the pupils have difficulties with a newly-met expression or word and make sense of what is heard in terms of previously known sounds and words.

Does scientific training overcome this common tendency to anticipate and interpret what we see? There is no evidence that it does so, only that anticipations are more directed and heightened. Picture a research scientist checking on the effects of a newly developed drug on laboratory animals. Prior knowledge will suggest that certain organs, e.g. the liver, will be the first to show adverse effects and microscope slides of tissue removed from these vulnerable organs might be examined. Evidence will be sought for known abnormalities, e.g. enlargement, atrophy or distortion of particular cells, or indications that the cell walls have developed inadequately, and so forth. A toxic drug which generates familiar abnormalities will soon be detected but the problem lies with the toxic material whose action is unusual and unanticipated. The importance of perceiving the unexpected is demonstrated in an incident in the work of Anna Brito. June Goodfield describes the situation:

Lymphocyte destruction naturally occurs in all animals that have had a viral or other infection. In such cases one *expects* to see empty areas in the lymph nodes. But Anna had been sharp enough to spot similar empty areas in the tissues of *healthy* thymectomized mice, where gross cell destruction would not be expected to have occurred. This was a puzzling clue . . .[5]

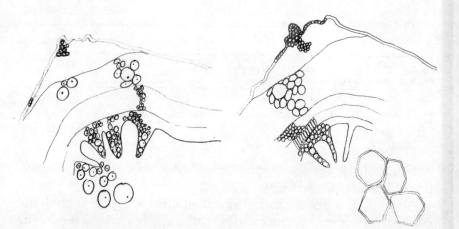

Fig. 1.3 Perceptions before and after instruction.

Source: C.G. Carré and J.O. Head, *Through the Eyes of the Pupil*, McGraw-Hill (UK), 1974

We can see the importance of prior knowledge affecting perception from the drawings shown in Fig. 1.3. On the left hand side are shown the observations of a sixth form science student examining plant tissue through a microscope. Later, after receiving some instruction on the topic, he made the drawing shown on the right of the same tissue. In each case the visual stimuli must have been the same, but the ability to interpret changed.

Very few well recorded accidental or serendipitious discoveries in science were totally unanticipated. Fleming had been looking for something like penicillin long before the *Penicillium* spores were by chance carried onto his culture dish. Newton had been thinking about gravity and the solar system before taking note of the falling apple and postulating what would happen if the apple tree was thought to extend into space. The old maxim that 'chance favours the prepared mind' has much force.

Not only can the idea of an absolute scientific objectivity be attacked on psychological grounds, but also because it ignores the context in which a person works. We carry with us concepts and beliefs derived from our particular culture and these tend to limit our ability to imagine alternative possibilities. For example, an issue of debate among historians is the extent to which it would have been possible for an individual in sixteenth century Europe to have been an atheist. The contemporary debate was about the nature of God and the role of the church, and all the protagonists assumed the existence of God. The phenomenon of simultaneous discovery in science, e.g. with the discovery of calculus, or with Wallace and Darwin postulating evolution, lends support to belief in the importance of socio-cultural factors. Only when a community is ready to accept a particular new idea will it be 'discovered'.[6]

In view of all these criticisms we might wonder why the belief in scientific objectivity has survived. There are two possible contributory factors: firstly a misunderstanding of a perfectly sound case, and secondly a strong emotional commitment to the belief.

The common misunderstanding arises with respect to how we recognise the truth or value of someone's work. In science the test is an experiment in which personal feelings and cultural attitudes act as a hindrance rather than a help. In the humanities the subjective influence plays a more positive and constructive role. Ultimately, what tests have we of the worthwhileness of a painting or a piece of music, other than our personal emotional response to it? That idea does not deny the role of the intellect in helping us to understand and appreciate the arts, but the argument goes that in this instance the intellect has to act as a facilitator, not as the arbitrator. A person's religious and political beliefs, personal interests and life-style, may well affect his or her work as a historian, sociologist or literary critic, but it would hardly affect work as a chemist.

Furthermore, attempts to impose onto scientists an outside belief system incompatible with the available scientific evidence, as with the Inquisition and Galileo, or the church in the last century over evolution, or more recently, the Lysenko affair, have all led to the discredit and discomfiture of those attempting to make that imposition. A strong case can be made for the relative objective nature of science, but it is wrong to claim complete objectivity.

Confusion has come from misunderstanding some philosophers of science. For example, Popper's stress on the value of objective knowledge has been interpreted as an argument that science proceeds, or ought to proceed, solely through the exercise of objective thinking. That view distorts his position, for, despite the title of his book: *The Logic of Scientific Discovery*[7] he was not concerned with the process of creative discovery at all but solely with the next stage, in which the scientific community assesses the worth of a claim to discovery. He argued that worthwhile scientific theories should yield hypotheses which are open to test and refutation by empirical experiment, and that in that testing process the open, objective mind is necessary. Even in that context Popper was being essentially prescriptive, suggesting the rules which scientists should follow, rather than descriptive, providing an account how scientists actually work.

A further factor contributing to the persistence of the belief in scientific objectivity comes from the strong emotional commitment of many scientists to that belief. It may sound ironic to talk of an emotional commitment to a belief in one's own objectivity, yet that paradox provides a key factor in understanding the psychology of science, a theme which will be developed later in this book.

The uncomfortable truth is that both scientific facts and theories merely represent a particular world view, a model which we hold of the world. One might wish to argue that it is a fact that when a candle burns, oxygen in the air combines with the elements in the hydrocarbon to yield water and carbon dioxide. But in the eighteenth century it was an accepted fact that the burning candle was emitting phlogiston. Thirty years ago we were told that noble gases did not form chemical compounds, now we are told as a fact that they do.

What we regard as being factually true is in reality a model employed to make sense of our observations of the universe. Sometimes the observations may change as, for example, when new detecting instruments are developed revealing more details about outer space or about microscopically small structures. However, in the case of the burning candle there have been no changes in observation and we regard the facts as being different because the prevailing theories which we use have changed. The fact that different explanatory theories can be derived from the same observed effects demonstrates that theories are not simply the direct logical consequence of considering the evidence: there is an intervention of the human mind, so that all theories are creations of that mind.

We might want to argue that even if facts are in reality theory-laden then at least our observations themselves are neutral. But is that really so? When, for example, I look at an instrument and report the observation that one amp is flowing through the circuit I am confusing two components of the story. What I actually observe is the movement of a needle, a spot of light, or a digital read-out. In transforming that observation into the description of the current flow I am subscribing to certain theories which underlie the design and calibration of the instrument. One of the most notorious examples of falling into that particular trap comes from the experiment for school pupils to 'verify' Ohm's Law using the conventional voltmeter and ammeter. The crucial point is that these instruments have been constructed on the basis that Ohm's Law is operating, hence we have become locked into a circular argument.

We can, of course, push this argument about the cultural relativism of science to absurd limits arguing that as all facts and theories are in no absolute sense true we might as well choose to believe in any one theory as another, so there is no value in the

9

received knowledge of conventional science. But conventional scientific views are conventional because they have withstood certain tests over a period of time; to be accepted theories need to be compatible with our observations, they need to make sense of these observations and they need to be consistent. Viewed in those terms our contemporary views are highly developed and sophisticated and will usually prove more useful than naive alternatives.

Nevertheless there is a danger that we allow ourselves to slide from thinking that reality is *like* some model to arguing that it *is* that model in an absolute sense. I often detect such confusion among students when dealing with the dual nature of light. However carefully I may explain that both the electromagnetic and photon descriptions are no more than models of reality students will often ask, 'What is light really like?' The question reveals a belief that the teacher knows the answer but for some reason is being coy in providing it.

That question about light's dual nature provides an illustration of a key issue in handling these models: that is, a recognition of the limit to the usefulness of each model. It is convenient to think in terms of electromagnetic radiation when considering the propagation of light, including reflection, refraction and interference, and it is convenient to think in terms of photons when considering the generation and absorption of light, for example the photoelectric effect. One answer to the students should be that neither model is in any absolute sense correct but it is convenient to use a particular model to help understand a specific phenomenon.

The Psychological Evidence

The suggestion that science makes a particular cognitive demand for its mastery, a theme which will be developed in the next chapter, will probably cause little surprise, for science is usually regarded as difficult to study. The possibility that there might be a particular set of affective demands may be less obvious, nevertheless the evidence is overwhelming, albeit initially somewhat confusing. One of the main problems is to handle a wide variety of data gathered over the last fifty years through the employment of many different enquiry techniques. The variety can be illustrated by contrasting the well-known pioneering studies of Louis Terman and Anne Roe in the United States.

Terman was concerned with the characteristics of highly intelligent people. In the early 1920s he identified, through the use of paper and pencil intelligence tests, 1528 school pupils in California who represented the top one per cent of the school population. These pupils were subjected to a battery of further tests concerned with a wide range of psychological factors and also with such issues as family background and physical health. Follow-up studies were made at approximately ten year intervals so that a longitudinal profile was developed. Arising from this project, Terman[8] made a comparative study of 800 gifted males of whom 284 were scientists, using this term to include engineers and medical practitioners. He found a number of definite differences between the scientists and the control group, including childhood behaviour, social adjustment and adult leisure interests.

The use of psychometric tests to explore differences between sub-groups of a population, such as scientists and non-scientists within a student population, is common. Terman's work, however, remains unusual both in its scale and more importantly in its longitudinal character. Usually, information about home background and childhood behaviour is gained from reminiscence, which is always somewhat suspect, whereas greater credence can be given to Terman's contemporary evidence, particularly to his assertion that the difference between the scientists and others was already clearly evident in the school pupils when they were first identified at an average age of eleven.

Another early worker in this field, Anne Roe, looked at highly creative scientists and gave lengthy interviews, accompanied by clinical tests, to 22 physical scientists, 20 biologists and 22 social scientists, all men of great eminence in their field.[9] She too found that the male scientists had clear personality characteristics which will be outlined in Chapter 4.

The striking feature to emerge was that despite their differences in methods and subjects, Terman and Roe arrived at very similar findings and conclusions. It is true that Anne Roe took note of Terman's findings in designing her test battery, but the differences in methodologies remained. Furthermore later work has tended to confirm and extend their results rather than contradict them.

A newer and totally different approach can be found in the use of psychometric personality tests, such as those developed by Cattell and Eysenck. The need for such tests was made by Cattell with the comment:

There is not a single measurement in the work of Pierre Janet, Sigmund Freud, Alfred Adler, and Carl Jung . . . with theories often based on a description of a single case and where the very description failed to agree with that by others.

Although Cattell himself took note of ideas drawn from clinical work and the use of projective tests, he was the key figure in the development of paper and pencil psychometric tests of personality. From data drawn from three sources – interviews, questionnaires, and performance tests – Cattell identified sixteen primary personality factors: further secondary factors can be derived from these sixteen. Over the years, however, there has been a growing criticism of this work but nevertheless the 'Cattell 16 PF test', and its derivatives for younger people, are still widely employed, particularly in the United States.

In Britain the work of Eysenck has had more influence. He identified two key dimensions to personality: extroversion–introversion and neuroticism–stability, these two dimensions being independent.[10]

These psychometric tests have been extensively employed to explore the relationship between personality factors and academic achievement but not all these studies have kept the data from different subject groups separate. However, relevant information can be found in a detailed study of undergraduates drawn from seven British universities by Entwistle and Wilson.[11] They identified two groups of students who were highly successful. These were:

1 highly-motivated, stable, conservative, tough-minded scientists, mainly male;
2 hardworking, syllabus-free arts students drawn from middle-class homes.

They also noted personality differences between undergraduates drawn from different departments. Clear patterns were found, with the scientists being more syllabus-bound, more conservative, and less neurotic than students drawn from the humanities and social sciences.

The in-depth study of a few distinguished scientists by Anne Roe and the use of psychometric tests with large student populations by Entwistle and Wilson illustrate the range of evidence which has to be considered. In surveying such a range Fisch gloomily commented:

Lacking integration, substantive research in the field has been spasmodic, discontinuous and fragmentary, largely bereft of any cohesive concepts or systematic pursuit of questions and methodologies.[12]

It is hoped that in this book some cohesive concepts will be developed so that the mass of material can be rendered sensible.

The Psychological Context

The failure previously, to generate a sound theoretical base for this work which Fisch sought, can be partly attributed to the modes of psychological enquiry which have been dominant. Early this century different schools of psychology got locked into fierce debate which was rarely informed by empirical evidence. The rise of behaviourism was an inevitable response, accentuated by the demand in the second world war for techniques of classifying and training service personnel. The net effect was to shift attention from the totality of the individual person to those discrete aspects which could be studied systematically within the scientific paradigm. Aspects of perception, learning, motor skills, and so forth, were studied in isolation; the methodology was such that all factors other than the one under scrutiny were assumed to be held constant. The advantage of techniques within this model is that the results are likely to be reliable. The disadvantage is that they are equally likely to be trivial. If we consider that psychology tends to lead either to precise statements about minor matters, or vague statements about important issues, then for several decades greater value was placed on the former.

Since about 1970 there has been a growing reaction against this dominant mode of thinking. It has been increasingly realised that while psychometric tests may yield reliable evidence which help confirm or deny existing hypotheses they rarely provide new insights. Doubt has been expressed as to whether the physical science paradigm should really be the only model for psychologists. The historian, for example, like the psychologist, is concerned with the production of accurate accounts of the dynamics of human behaviour. History, too, has a rigour, albeit different from that of science and possibly more relevant to much of psychology.

This trend in psychology has shifted the level of analysis back to that of the totality of the individual person. It has been especially influential in cognitive psychology where ideas about motivation, cognitive structures, learning, and so forth, have undergone dramatic changes, some of which will be described later. On the affective side this new thinking has been slower to take root but one can now detect a renewed interest in the ways individuals make sense of their world, and later in this book some new ideas about the impact of science on the individual will be offered.

Notes and References

1 J. Ziman *Public Knowledge: The Social Dimension of Science*, Cambridge University Press 1968.
2 J.D. Watson *The Double Helix*, Weidenfeld and Nicholson (London) 1968.
3 'Fable: A Lost Child Keeping Warm' appears in G.C. Pimentel (ed) *Chemistry: An Experimental Science*, W.H. Freeman (San Francisco) 1963, pages 3–4. The students are introduced to the inductive method in science by the story of a child who has to light a fire to keep warm. After finding that logs and wooden handles burn the child creates a hypothesis that cylindrical objects burn. The experience on the next night when the child tried to burn a metal pipe and a glass bottle demonstrated the error of that hypothesis and its replacement by a more useful one. Science, it is suggested, proceeds by trial, the making and modification of hypotheses in this fashion.
4 P.B. Medawar, *Induction and Intuition in Scientific Thought*, Methuen (London) 1969
5 J. Goodfield *An Imagined World*, Hutchinson (London) 1981, page 27. June Goodfield, a zoologist, wrote this account of how a scientist actually works after five years observing Anna Brito. The importance of the mental anticipation in observation is confirmed by Anna Brito's comment quoted in that book: 'I missed those flourescing cells. I missed them because I was not looking for them. Now I am,

and I see them. But they were there all the time.' (page 116). For an account of perception see R.L. Gregory *Eye and Brain*, Weidenfeld and Nicholson (London) 1966.

6   That perspective on scientific discovery is developed by A. Brannigan *The Social Basis of Scientific Discoveries* Cambridge University Press 1981.

7   K.R. Popper, *The Logic of Scientific Discovery*, Hutchinson (London) 1968.

8   L.M. Terman, 'Are scientists different?', *Scientific American*, Volume 192 (1955) pages 25–29.

9   A. Roe, *The Making of a Scientist*, Dodd, Mead and Co. (New York) 1952.

10 The characteristics of an extrovert being impulsiveness and sociability, whereas the introvert would be more cautious and self-contained. Eysenck's *neuroticism* corresponds to what the layperson, and many other psychologists would label as being anxious, his 'normal' person being someone relaxed and calm. More recently he has added a *psychotism* scale to the test but that is only relevant in clinical situations. A controversial figure, Eysenck has been the most widely known British psychologist in recent years, exercising considerable influence. His work on personality and its measurement has been his main achievement.

11 N.J. Entwistle, and J.D. Wilson, *Degrees of Excellence: The Academic Achievement Game*, Hodder and Stoughton (London) 1977.

12 R. Fisch, 'Psychology of science' in I. Spiegel-Rosing, and D.de S. Price, *Science, Technology and Society: A Cross-Disciplinary Perspective*, Sage (London) 1977, page 277.

2

The Cognitive Demand

We might agree that not everyone has the potential to become a professional scientist, or even do well at science in school. To what extent are the limitations of individual cognitive ability the crucial determinant of choice and success? Do adolescents simply choose those subjects for which they possess the most aptitude and is success solely determined by that aptitude? That possibility, however, fails to explain the association of certain personality characteristics with an interest in science, as described in Chapter 4. Nevertheless the role of cognitive influences needs to be considered.

Evidence from Intelligence Testing

We might start with considering the evidence drawn from the use of intelligence tests because this mode of testing has a long history and an extensive literature. The prime use of such tests has been to screen and select populations so that the ablest can be identified for specific purposes, and they fulfil that function reasonably adequately when dealing with a wide spread of ability. If, for example, it were suggested that someone with an IQ of 100, the national mean, had achieved success at university we would assume that there had been a test error, or that the particular undergraduate course must be suspect. Yet if we look at academic success among a selected population, such as university undergraduates, we find that the correlation between success and measured intelligence is slight.[1] The apparent incompatibility of this evidence is usually accounted for in terms of there being a crucial threshold, so that a certain minimum cognitive ability is required for success with a particular task; provided that minimum is achieved then essentially success will be determined by other factors, such as diligence. As the measured intelligence of science students tends to be slightly higher than for those in other subject areas the threshold may be slightly higher in science, but the effect may be an artifact of the tests which assess a type of thinking more akin to that experienced in science. For science undergraduates the crucial threshold seems to be about 110–115 IQ points.

Interesting differences in the cognitive biases in intelligence were found in a study of 315 schoolboys aged 15–16, specialising in a variety of disciplines. From an intelligence test plus tests of vocabulary, general knowledge, and spatial ability the pattern shown in Table 2.1 was found.

Table 2.1 Biases in intelligence test results linked with subject choice (for schoolboys)

	General intelligence	Accuracy	Spatial ability	Vocabulary	General knowledge	Cognitive bias
Classics	f	vg	g	vg	f	none
Modern languages	f	f	f	w	f	verbal
History	p	w	p	f	f	verbal
Physical sciences	vg	g	vg	f	f	numerical and spatial
Biological sciences	f	f	f	w	f	none

p = poor, w = weak, f = fair, g = good, vg = very good

Source: L. Hudson, *The Relation of Psychological Test Scores to Academic Bias*, British Journal of Educational Psychology, 33, (1963), pages 120–131 Scottish Academic Press Ltd. (Edinburgh)

The overall bias among the schoolboys within the different subject groups is indicated in the last column. Similar biases were found by Entwistle and Wilson with the verbal and mathematical aptitude scores of first year undergraduates. The figures given in Table 2.2 indicate the standard mean scores for each group (that is the difference between the mean for that group and the mean for the total student population divided by the weighted means of the standard deviations).

17

Table 2.2 Cognitive aptitude scores for undergraduates

	Verbal	Mathematical
English	0.65	−0.63
French	0.33	−0.73
History	−0.01	−0.68
Economics	−0.07	−0.22
Sociology	0.25	−0.37
Biology	−0.26	0.01
Chemistry	−0.25	0.59
Physics	−0.11	0.91
Engineering	−0.21	0.59
Mathematics	−0.20	1.39

Source: N.J. Entwistle and J.D. Wilson, *Degrees of Excellence: The Academic Achievement Game*, Hodder and Stoughton, 1977

A crude measure of general intelligence can be obtained from the sum of these two scores and to take one example, it will be seen that physicists emerge with a higher score than historians.

Piagetian Studies

The body of work carried out by Piaget and his team in Geneva has had much more impact on science education. Piaget attempted to explain the variety of human behaviour in terms of a limited number of fundamental structural features, and he postulated qualitative differences in forms of knowledge which could be described and distinguished by symbolic logic. Each individual person in maturing develops the mental capacity to handle increasingly difficult forms of knowledge. The rate of maturation varies between individuals but the same path would be followed in developing through the hierarchical sequence.

Perhaps the aspect of the Piagetian description of most concern to science education is the progress from concrete operational thinking to formal operational thinking, a change which Piaget saw as allowing individuals to think more in abstract and complex ways, and which he suggested characteristically develops in early adolescence. The actual examples quoted by Inhelder and Piaget[2] in their description of the development of formal operational thinking came from the physical sciences, e.g. chemical combinations, the pendulum, the inclined plane, and so forth. For that reason this work has an immediate appeal to science educators. By comparing a particular curriculum to the descriptions given by Inhelder and Piaget it is possible to attach labels to each topic indicating its cognitive demand. If we also measure the cognitive abilities of the pupils we might then check whether the curriculum material has been correctly matched for its intended population. In that way we have been given a clear guide to the selection and sequencing of science topics for the school curriculum.

These ideas were taken up in the construction of new curriculum material, e.g. the Nuffield 5 to 13 Project, and in dealing with apparent difficulties with existing published curricula. For example, when the Nuffield O level chemistry scheme was revised in the early 1970s the treatment of the mole concept was modified by Ingle and Shayer[3] in the light of Piagetian type analysis which suggested that parts of the previous scheme placed too great a demand on pupils, a conclusion supported by the evidence of teachers' reports and by analysis of examination answers.

This early work took the published Piagetian ideas as received wisdom and it was only in the mid-1970s that Shayer and his colleagues at Chelsea carried out a large scale systematic check.[4] That group attempted three tasks. The first was to develop tests which could be used in class situations, Piaget's original work having been with individual interviews, a technique precluding study of large populations. Once these Science Reasoning Tests had been developed then the population norms could be found. Finally curricula could be analysed to see if they were appropriate for the target population.

Perhaps the most striking finding was that far fewer adolescents developed formal operational thinking than Piaget's original work suggested. Fig. 2.1 indicates the proportion at different ages.

The implication of such findings is that less than half the school population at the age of 15 can handle the abstract concepts typically found in traditional O level syllabuses, and frequently reproduced in CSE examinations.

Recently, however, the Piagetian work has been widely criticised and it is by no means easy to assess how well it will stand up in the face of these attacks. It might help the analysis to see this

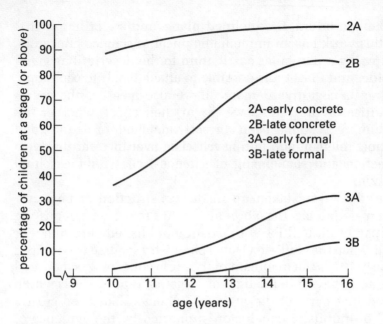

Fig. 2.1 Proportion of children at different Piagetian stages in a representative British child population

Source: M. Shayer and P. Adey, *Towards a Science of Science Teaching,* Heinemann Educational Books, 1981

work in relation to the understanding of science being at three levels: the descriptions of what children can and cannot do, second order explanations or theories about these empirical findings, and a synthesising meta-theory. An analogy can be made with chemistry where we have descriptions of reactions, second order explanations in terms of acids and bases, or redox reactions and so forth, and finally, a meta-theory in terms of the behaviour of atoms, electrons and ions.

How does Piaget's work stand up at these three levels? In general, replication exercises have confirmed that children under the test conditions behave much as he described, other than the finding already mentioned, that fewer adolescents develop formal operational thinking than had been assumed.

At the meta-theory level there is considerable disquiet about Piaget's work. There has been concern that he assumed one cor-

20

rect way of acquiring knowledge and ignored the possibility of alternative routes. We might note, however, that these criticisms of the meta-theory do not discredit the other two levels. To pursue the analogy with chemistry, if we chose to abandon our usual models of the atom and electron and adopted another model, for example in terms of quarks, that would not affect the way reagents react with each other.

The most relevant and telling criticism is at the middle level. Although it is agreed that children do not successfully carry out certain Piagetian tasks at a given age it can be argued that the difficulty arises from causes outside the actual logic of the task. Their unfamiliarity with the materials, inability to understand the verbal instruction and the limitations of their memory might be crucial. It has been pointed out that given the right conditions young children are capable of much more sophisticated thought than one would usually anticipate.[5] The really crucial point with reference to science education is to what extent a person's existing range of cognitive strategies is simply limited by prior experience, which can be compensated for, or by a genetically determined stage of mental development which cannot be modified.

It should be possible to find evidence to illuminate that issue by giving students a variety of tests on different topics and seeing whether their performances are consistent at some cognitive level. A number of such studies have been made, but unfortunately they have yielded conflicting evidence. Even more unfortunately, protagonists in debate about the value of Piaget's work tend to quote only from those studies most sympathetic to their own viewpoint, so effective communication has been minimised.

One danger in this situation is to allow the argument to become polarised between the two extreme viewpoints when it is likely the truth lies somewhere in the middle. Some topics in science and mathematics are likely to be inherently more difficult to handle than others and children may experience considerable problems in the more difficult areas. For example, children seem to find multiplying much more difficult than addition and will often employ an addition strategy when asked to multiply. Thus when asked to multiply five by six they may add up a pattern of six dots on a piece of paper five times over. Initially that strategy will work but later on it will fail, leaving them in considerable confusion.

Similarly it appears that the concept of *rate* is not too easy to understand but the idea of *changes in rates*, as in acceleration, is most difficult. Psychological difficulties do not correspond exactly to the scientific logical development of the subject. The sequence velocity–acceleration–force is a logical one in physics with each term being dimensionally more complex than its predecessor. In practice, however, students find it easier to gain some understanding of force than they do of acceleration. The fact that forces can be 'felt' as a push or pull might facilitate understanding while the use of the accelerator pedal in a car only compounds the confusion as they can gain the impression that the more the pedal is depressed the greater will be the resultant acceleration.

Although we might agree that some concepts are inherently more difficult than others there is ample evidence from cross-cultural studies that understanding is influenced by personal experience. For example, children who play a role in the family economy by scavenging for food or fuel acquire the concepts of classification of these materials at a very early age, earlier than Piagetian analysis would suggest.

The essential issue is to what extent academic performance is limited by inadequate or inappropriate experience. Can teachers develop intervention stategies to markedly improve the level of pupils' understanding or have teachers already achieved the optimum results? As yet there have been few attempts to directly explore that question.

The Constructivist Perspective

The main opposition group to the Piagetian position in relation to science education comes from the 'constructivists', a term referring back to the work of Kelly on personal construct theory.[6] Kelly stressed the importance of the individual way we make sense of the world. He suggested that we are naturally mentally active and develop a set of personal constructs based on our experience of the world, with which we anticipate how people and things behave.

There have been claims that a constructivist approach to education might be valuable and much recent research in science education has been within this paradigm. Some workers accept the totality of Kelly's theories and methodologies, for example, the use of repertory grids to ascertain someone's constructs on a given topic, while others under the constructivist banner only share a basic orientation, that of viewing people as actively developing constructs which shape behaviour and understanding.

Although there is still some uncertainty about the precise importance of the individual's prior experience to learning, the clear trend in recent work has been to place more and more emphasis on this factor. Ausubel's famous comment: 'If I had to reduce all of educational psychology to just one principle, I would say this: <u>The most important single factor influencing learning is</u> <u>what the learner already knows.</u> Ascertain this and teach him accordingly',[7] has been increasingly accepted. The reasons for this shift in opinion are numerous but one influence has been the growing recognition among cognitive psychologists that we need to consider learning in context. The quality of learning experienced by an individual will be influenced both by the actual content of the learning experience and also by the situation in which the learning takes place, so that the content can be recalled later through the contextual setting. It is a familiar experience that hearing a piece of music may bring back memories of the situation in which it was first heard and so similarly the content of the lesson will be stored in the memory alongside the context, e.g. the voice and manner of the teacher. This emphasis on the content and context of learning has clearly diminished the importance to be attached to generalised descriptions of learning abilities, such as those of Piaget.

This alternative approach is valuable in its suggestion of teaching strategies. The assumption is that all pupils hold some personal view of a topic prior to it being taught and the idea of the *tabula rasa* is rejected. In that event learning can be blocked or delayed by this prior belief if it is not compatible with the new material to be learnt.

In the light of this description of learning it is scarcely surprising that at long last considerable effort is being made to develop investigatory techniques to discover what children actually believe about science topics prior to receiving formal lessons on these topics. Errors are being treated as informative rather than merely incorrect.

The next stages are clearly more difficult. No teacher can elicit

23

and take account of the different views of, say, a hundred pupils on a range of science topics. Some organising principle is needed for classification. One such principle comes from finding that children often seem to hold ideas about science which closely resemble those held by the educated population in past ages, thus they may hold a pre-Newtonian view of mechanics. The coincidence of views is not surprising if one remembers that the beliefs held by previous cultures made sense within certain limits. Common experience might suggest that heavy objects fall faster under gravity than light objects, that the sun goes round the earth, and so forth. Newtonian and allied classical physics may sometimes seem to be contrary to common sense; certainly the developments in physics this century, such as the theory of relativity, often seem to be at total variance with everyday experience. We can see why ontongenesis, the development of ideas within an individual, may follow a similar path to phylogenesis, the development of ideas within a community.

That link with the history of science has further value as it suggests a possible mechanism to produce change, i.e. learning, in an individual. If, for the moment, I accept Kuhn's description of the nature of science development,[8] then I can argue that learning by an individual may be compared to a paradigm shift among a group of scientists. Scientists will initially work within a particular paradigm until the weight of discordant evidence can no longer be accommodated by merely tinkering with that paradigm and a totally new model has to be sought, as when the idea of phlogiston was abandoned, or when plate tectonics were conceived. If, by analogy, a student holds a view which I would regard as incorrect, then a tactic to produce meaningful change is to offer evidence which is incompatible with the view being held. The consequent dissonance might generate a willingness to seek a new model despite the mental turmoil that change may involve.

How useful might this constructivist approach be? Until recently most of the effort has been in establishing that pupils do hold these alternative conceptions prior to formal science teaching.[9] The evidence for the existence of these prior beliefs is now abundant but the next need is to develop a descriptive pattern to these findings and detailed studies are required. For example, a promising line has been developed by Shipstone with reference to

24

pupils' ideas about current electricity.[10] It seems that the vast majority of pupils subscribe at some stage to a sequential model of direct current flow. With such a model the relative positions of a bulb and a resistance in series would affect the brightness with which the bulb is illuminated. If the current reaches the bulb first it will be fresh and have no reason to anticipate the resistance further along the circuit so it will light the bulb brightly. If, however, it reaches the resistance first, it will be exhausted by the effort of struggling through that and will only light the bulb weakly. Abler pupils hold this sequential model at about the age of 12 but two or three years later are beginning to accept the conventional physics explanation. The identification of such an alternative conception should suggest teaching tactics.

It will be noted that this constructivist view does not logically contradict Piaget's work. It may be the case that the sequential model of current electricity is a concrete operational model and only when a pupil develops formal operational thinking can the conventional explanation be understood.

Perhaps the weakest point in the constructivist argument is the belief that the production of empirical evidence which contradicts the individual's naive beliefs will produce dissonance, which in turn will lead on to learning. Unfortunately pupils can adopt other strategies to handle the conflict, such as by creating a division in the mind between school knowledge, given by the teacher and required for examinations, and 'real' knowledge about the outside world. That division can often be identified, e.g. when a pupil argues that a chair is not made up from elements, compounds or mixtures, as these terms refer to chemicals and a chair is not a chemical. Another possibility is that the pupil puts up a block to the conflicting evidence, e.g. by saying, 'I cannot understand science', a statement which is likely to be self-fulfilling as it inhibits making the effort to understand.

The crucial point is that changing one's mind is not just a cognitive act. It involves abandoning the security provided by the previous way of making sense of the world and entering the confusion of the unknown before reaching the new belief. The readiness to undergo that experience is likely to be determined by personality factors more than purely cognitive ones.

Cognitive Style

That comment on mental flexibility leads to a consideration of the cognitive style of an individual. Many descriptions are given in the literature, including authoritarianism, cognitive complexity, field-dependence, cognitive control and impulsivity. The problem is to sort out whether these are all independent variables or not. This issue can be illustrated by looking at Hudson's work on convergency–divergency, but to understand that we need to go back to the story of the development of creativity tests.

In his famous address to the American Psychological Society in 1950, Guilford opened by saying

I discuss the subject of creativity with considerable hesitation for it represents an area in which psychologists generally, whether they be angels or not, have feared to tread.

Certainly prior to 1950, work on creativity tended to be solely psychoanalytical studies of individual highly creative persons. Both in this address, and later[11] Guilford suggested what might be the main characteristics of creative persons such as originality, flexibility, fluency and elaboration. His lead was followed in the late 1950s and early 1960s by a host of psychologists who, whether they were angels or not, generated psychometric tests of creativity. These differed from most other cognitive tasks in being essentially open-ended, seeking a variety of responses rather than the selection of one acceptable answer.

Their immediate relevance came from the study by Getzels and Jackson of students in one private high school in Chicago.[12] From somewhat meagre evidence Getzels and Jackson suggested that a distinction could be made between convergers, who did relatively well at the conventional tests but poorly with the open-ended tests, and divergers who showed the reverse bias. They argued that the latter group were frequently disadvantaged at school as neither the curriculum nor the teachers gave these students opportunities to develop and display their particular forte.

The Getzels and Jackson study met considerable criticism, because the creativity tests correlated so badly with each other, because the work was done with an atypical population (the pupils in that particular school had an average IQ of 130) and because replication studies have yielded conflicting evidence. Nevertheless the Getzels and Jackson study had a considerable impact on other psychologists. Hudson had been working on the cognitive differences between schoolboys within different subjects, as noted earlier, then turned his attentions to the relationship between convergent and divergent tendencies and subject choice, arguing that the scientists were the most convergent.

We might notice a marked change in tone between Hudson's opening sentence, 'The aim of this book is to delineate two types of clever schoolboy: the converger and the diverger',[13] and his note of caution two years later when he argued, 'Yet even at the outset I was not pigeon-holing. No one was, or was ever expected to be, consistently convergent or consistently divergent.'[14] In view of the widespread influence of his ideas on convergency and a bias towards science we need to look carefully at this shift of opinion.

One objection to the original Hudson work is that it was based solely on studies of English schoolboys in the pre-Nuffield era. One might describe the traditional school science curricula as exercises in convergent thinking so that it is hardly surprising that more convergers opted for such courses. But what about science at other levels? Cropley, in a study of Australian students, showed that in their fourth year at university, which was largely spent on project work, divergers were the most successful in science.[15] Even more damaging were the findings that the scores for the creativity tests were very dependent on test conditions and instructions. It had been previously assumed that a low score on these tests came from a lack of imagination, a failure to think of a variety of responses. However, it was later found that if the test instructions were modified so that the subjects were invited to respond not as themselves, but in the imagined role of a highly creative person, then many of the lowest scoring persons became highly productive. The inference is that convergency is not simply a product of a deficient imagination but is a consequence of a self-censoring process. The converger sets up some rules in his or her mind, asking perhaps whether each possibility is feasible or socially acceptable, before responding. Hence convergency is an expression of rule-obeying behaviour. The importance of that interpretation is that it links Hudson's work with that previously described in the literature on attitudes to authority and being syllabus-bound.

The fact that we might now interpret Hudson's findings in terms of an explanatory model other than that he originally proposed should not obscure the point that he had identified significant differences between students opting for science and the others. Such findings still need to be explained, and the possibility of authoritarianism being relevant shifts the discussion from the purely cognitive into the area of personality and resultant attitudes.

In fact many links can be made between aspects of cognitive style and personality. For example, Witkin's work on field dependence and independence is widely accepted as having identified an important factor in cognitive performance. Starting from his initial work with subjects needing to orientate themselves in a tilted room, a more general factor has been identified, that of identifying the key issues in a complex problem free from various distractors. The reported correlation between field independence and various forms of academic achievement may cause no surprise, but Witkin himself suggested that field independence was linked to the development of a personal identity, which in turn was associated with relationships with parents in early childhood. He commented:

This sketchy overview has sought to demonstrate that cognitive functioning is intimately related to personality. In fact it is sometimes hard to tell where cognition ends and personality begins.[16]

Perhaps that quotation provides a good basis for summarising this chapter. The evidence from the use of both intelligence tests and Piagetian science reasoning tests suggests that many science concepts are not readily accessible to the total school population. It is still in dispute whether that limitation is genetically determined, and so cannot be altered but merely allowed for, as many Piagetians would argue, or can be minimised by the appropriate pedagogic strategies, as constructivists would argue. The constructivist approach holds out a hope of making science more accessible but the extent of the improvement has yet to be demonstrated. In any event the main factor inhibiting success in handling science may well lie in the domain of the affective rather than the cognitive. It may be necessary for success that the curriculum material is within the competence of the learner, but that is not a sufficient condition to ensure success. There is every reason to believe, on the basis of cognitive test scores, that for every person already studying science many more could cope. The limitation seems to be a lack of interest, a feeling that science is not suitable, useful or relevant. Science does seem to make a particular cognitive demand in terms of the cognitive styles employed in its mastery but, as Witkin reminded us, cognitive styles are largely shaped by the personality of the individual.

Notes and References

1 For example, L. Hudson, 'Future open Scholars', *Nature*, Volume 202 (1964) page 834, and J.B. Gibson and P. Light, 'Intelligence among university students', *Nature*, Volume 213 (1967) page 441.

2 B. Inhelder and J. Piaget *The Growth of Logical Thinking*, Routledge and Kegan Paul (London) 1958.

3 R.B. Ingle and M. Shayer, 'Conceptual demands of Nuffield O level chemistry', *Education in Chemistry*, Volume 8 (1971) page 182.

4 M. Shayer and P. Adey, *Towards a Science of Science Teaching*, Heinemann Educational Books (London) 1981.

5 For example, P. Bryant, *Perception and Understanding in Young Children*, Methuen (London) 1974 and M. Donaldson, *Children's Minds*, Fontana (London) 1978.

6 G.A. Kelly, *The Psychology of Personal Constructs*, Norton (New York) 1955. Kelly's own writings are not that easy to master but a good introduction to his theory is provided in D. Bannister and F. Fransella, *Inquiring Man*, Penguin (Harmondsworth) 1971.

7 D.P. Ausubel, *Educational Psychology: A Cognitive View*, Holt, Rinehart and Winston (New York) 1968, page iv.

8 T.S. Kuhn, *The Structure of Scientific Revolutions*, University of Chicago Press 1962.

9 Examples can be found in W.F. Archenhold *et al. Cognitive Development Research in Science and Mathematics*, University of Leeds Press 1980.

10 D.M. Shipstone, *A Study of Secondary School Pupils' Understanding of Current, Voltage and Resistance in Simple D.C. Circuits*, University of Nottingham 1982.

11 J.P. Guilford, 'Traits of creativity' in P.E. Vernon *Creativity*, Penguin (Harmondsworth) 1970 pages 167–188.

12 J.W. Getzels and P.W. Jackson *Creativity and Intelligence*, Wiley (New York) 1962.
13 L. Hudson, *Contrary Imaginations*, Methuen (London) 1966.
14 L. Hudson, *Frames of Mind*, Methuen (London) 1968 page 91.
15 A.J. Cropley, 'Divergent thinking and science specialists' *Nature* Volume 215 (1967) pages 671–672.
16 H.A Witkin, 'Some implications of research on cognitive style for problems in education' in J.M. Whitehead, *Personality and Learning*, Hodder and Stoughton (London) 1975 page 302.

3

Attitudes, Images and Motivation

Underlying much of the discussion of cognitive demand in the last chapter was the issue of motivation. Both the ability to perform a task and a willingness to do so are necessary for success, the latter often proves the more important, and provides the theme for this chapter.

The Motivation to Learn

Until recently it has been a common assumption in psychology that people are naturally inert and passive and have to be provoked into action by some internal or external force. We find that belief common to psychoanalysts with their talk of the libido and to animal behaviourists with their experiments to ascertain whether thirst, hunger, sexual attraction or maternal care provide the strongest motivating force to take action. It has been appreciated only recently that this underlying assumption may be incorrect. Even the observation of animals reveals that when all their obvious physical needs have been fully satisfied they will often display active behaviour which has to be unsatisfactorily labelled 'play', or attributed to 'curiosity'. Children do not need to be motivated to learn, it seems to be a spontaneously occurring activity, at least until they are placed behind a desk in school and are told to learn something. Perhaps one should stop thinking about how a child learns a language in the first few years of life and ask instead how one can stop a child acquiring a language to which he or she has been exposed. Language acquisition, despite its difficulty, seems to be a natural and spontaneous activity among children. In sleep we all experience periods of dreaming at intervals throughout the night, so that sleep is far less passive than was once assumed. Perhaps the most striking demonstration of the need for continual

31

mental activity is with experiments in sensory deprivation in which subjects are placed in comfortable, but featureless environments, essentially a 'black box'. Far from enjoying the opportunity to be passive and do nothing, the experience usually proves most distressing to the subjects, who frequently report hallucinations and allied effects. Just as it is necessary for the heart to beat continuously in a living person, so that the cessation of the heartbeat is symptomatic of the end of life, so likewise it appears that the brain is continuously active. For about two-thirds of the day it needs to receive a variety of sensory inputs and throughout the 24 hours some active mental processes are occurring.

The question is not what causes someone to choose to learn rather than do nothing, but what causes a person to choose to concentrate on one particular activity, with its associated learning, in preference to an alternative activity with its associated learning. A full answer to that question will, it is to be hoped, emerge from the later chapters of this book, but we can anticipate some of the factors which are likely to affect motivation.

People are likely to pay attention and get involved in activities which they expect to be interesting, rewarding or worthwhile in some way. Previous experience, the expression of opinions by others, particularly peers, and the images generated by the media, will all serve as the basis for such beliefs.

Some images will be about science as a school subject and whether it might be beyond a person's intellectual competence, others will be about career opportunities and what working in a science based industry involves and some about scientists as people. All these have to be matched with the person's self-perception about their own abilities, interests and aptitudes. It will be in the light of these various beliefs, whether ill-informed or not, that career and subject choices will be made.

Images and Attitudes

A distinction can be made between these two terms. Images are mental pictures held in the conscious mind and so can be elicited by simple, direct means. For example, images held about about scientists can be ascertained by asking someone to describe a scientist, to invent an imaginary diary of a scientist, to select the more apposite from alternative descriptive adjectives referring to scientists, and so forth.

An attitude can be described as an underlying generalised construct. The fact that it is underlying suggests that the attitude may not simply be determined by direct questioning but much more subtle and searching methods are needed. Because we are dealing with a generalised idea it would be unreliable to try to determine attitudes from a few specific responses. Attitudes will be built up largely as a product of unique, individual experiences and each person will interpret evidence, anticipate events and make decisions in the light of the attitudes possessed. This effect on decision making is particularly crucial.

The literature on attitudes to science is extensive. These attitudes are seen as being important in their own right for their role in decision making processes and have also been extensively studied because attitudes seem to be more accessible to observation and measurement than personality variables. But, unlike the personality area, there have been few widely employed, standardised measures; instead many researchers have generated their own tests for a specific study, consequently comparisons between different sets of results are difficult. Even worse, many such tests have been poorly conceptualised in the first instance, partly because they have often had such flimsy bases in psychological theory. For example, a questionnaire might incorporate items testing beliefs on the material benefits to be gained from science, the value of science as a truth system, the difficulties involved in studying science, and so forth. If such data is all summated to yield a single score on a pro/anti-science continuum then scores, except those at the extreme ends of the scale, are almost impossible to interpret. Gardner[1] quotes instances of such ill-conceptualised measures. From the confusion in the literature we can, however, gain some usable information.

There is considerable evidence[2] that many school pupils have a stereotypical image of the scientist. A scientist is usually seen to be male, wearing a white coat and spectacles, is obsessively interested in science, unworldly, and unaware of persons and events outside science. Where does this image come from? Part may be from experience of some science teachers: certainly Hudson found striking differences in the imaginary diaries of science and arts teachers.[3] The former are shown as avoiding social contact with colleagues, resenting pupils other than able science sixth formers and wishing to spend leisure time in carrying out experiments in a home laboratory. In contrast the arts teacher is seen to enjoy social contacts and conversation, on the bus to school, with colleagues, with pupils during class discussion and at home.

These images may also be in part a creation of science fiction. Basalla[4] points out that science fiction presents two contrasting images of scientists. He, and that word is used in this context as more than a linguistic convention, is either an unworldly, remote figure who has to be protected from potential enemies and exploiters by younger assistants, the heroes in the tale, or he is a scheming, cunning man, obsessed with obtaining power over other people and seeking applications of science in unscrupulous ways as a means to that end. In both cases the scientist is somewhat unusual in his dealing with the world and other people. In both cases women tend to be seen in subordinate roles, often needing rescuing from some unpleasant fate by the heroes.

Science fiction is widely read and watched on television by teenagers and may have considerable influence, but that image would presumably be modified by their actual experience in working with science teachers. Science programmes on television provide another influence but with a few notable exceptions, such as the BBC series on the life of Darwin, these tend to say little about the persons involved in the events being described. Biographical information is rarely given about contemporary scientists.

Whatever their origin these stereotypical images are widely held. Hudson[5] found that pupils believed that: the male arts graduate was seen to be more likely to wear fashionable clothes (15.0 : 1), to flirt with his secretary (9.0 : 1) and be sociable (6.3 : 1) than the science graduate. By contrast the male science graduate was more likely to work long hours (14.5 : 1), to be faithful to his wife (4.6 : 1), to be competitive at work (2.2 : 1) and be embarrassed about sex (1.7 : 1).

Butcher[6] asked 300 Scottish schoolchildren, aged 13–14, to give their opinion about 15 professional careers. They were asked to comment on their own liking for such a career, the interest such work would hold for them, the salary they might earn, the prestige of that profession and the usefulness of the work to the community. It was found that boys exhibited a distinct liking for science at that age, with their first four choices in terms of liking a career being for science based professions. In contrast the only scientific career that appealed to the girls was medicine, their other top choices all being drawn from non-science areas. These pupils of 13 or so seem to have had fairly realistic views about the 'factual' items, those of salary and prestige, which suggests that they were well informed on these issues. It is noteworthy that although boys were attracted to science, and girls to teaching in general, neither sex was strongly attracted to science teaching.

After the age of 13 the boys' interest in science seemed to diminish. One study found that two-thirds of boys who placed a science subject or mathematics as their first choice at that age changed their mind before reaching the school leaving age.[7] Whitfield reports a similar finding in following the attitudes of 3490 pupils progressing from the third form through to the fifth form of secondary school. Interest in physics and chemistry rapidly declines in those two years, with boys and girls, although biology does not fare so badly, see Fig. 3.1. This change of interest might be an inevitable and natural consequence of the emergence of new values and beliefs in adolescence, but it ought to give some concern to science teachers. It has sometimes been claimed that the lack of science candidates to the universities is caused by school pupils receiving an inadequate exposure to these subjects, yet it can be argued that the more students meet science the less they like it.

This decline of interest appears to continue throughout the undergraduate years with science students, while with undergraduates in the arts and social sciences interest tends to increase.[8] The contemporary anti-science stance common among undergraduates seems to be related not only to the practical considerations of diminishing resources, pollution, and a failure to realise some of the more extravagant claims, e.g. by Bronowski in the early 1960s that 'Now we are in sight of having as much energy as we can need',[9] but also to science as a mode of enquiry and understanding. Keniston in a study of young North Americans suggests that many reject science as the attempt 'to analyse problems into manageable components', which is fraught with danger as

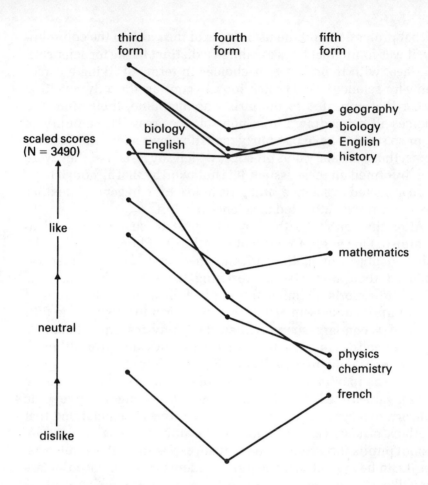

Fig. 3.1 Attitudes toward secondary school science subjects

Source: R.C. Whitfield, 'Educational Research and Science Teaching' *School Science Review*, Volume 60 (1979) pages 411–430. © R.C. Whitfield

'analysis almost inevitably involves reduction'. Students seek ideas beyond the instrumental values of science and challenge its concern for order, one student arguing 'the notion that man and nature are governed by regular laws is an illusion based on our insatiable desire for certainty'.[10]

In a British study of secondary school pupils Carré and Head[11] found the apparent lack of relevance of science being quoted against its study. For example, a boy of 14 wrote:

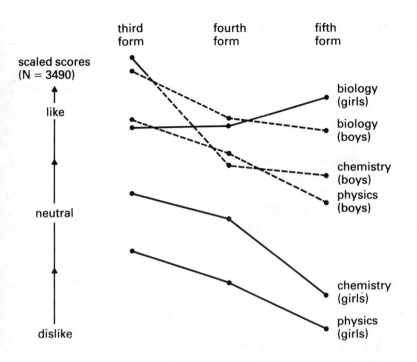

As it is, I sit at the back of the room listening to irrelevant rubbish on topics such as 'How to give yourself directional velocity if stuck in the middle of a frictionless ice-rink', and I am, not unnaturally, bored stiff. For God's sake give the subject some relevance.

One common complaint is that science has lost its appeal as an innovative adventurous activity. Selmes on the basis of his analysis of 50 hours of taped discussion with 12 and 13 year old pupils comments on the 'lack of realisation that there was any investigatory process in science; science was a body of knowledge to be "overcome" in one way or another.'[12] Writing as a head-master, Potts tells us of the attitudes of pupils aged 14 and 16 whom he interviewed in his school:

To the schoolchildren of this country it appears that science and technology have already solved most of our daily problems. The struggle is not to design an atomic power station but to persuade the miners' leaders to agree to it being constructed . . . . There is little curiosity about science: so much is now established fact. Techniques of science have become too careful to be exciting.'[13]

37

Attitudes and Subject Choice

Why do different pupils make different subject choices? We can imagine two possibilities. Either they have different perceptions about science and scientists so that they act differently in the light of these perceptions, or they may all share the same perceptions, but respond differently because they possess different self-images. An analogy can be made to a computer. Two computers yielding different outputs may receive different data inputs or, alternatively, possess different programs.

The answer seems to lie in an intermediate position between these two opposite hypotheses. It appears from the research evidence that to some extent pupils choosing science have a more positive image of science and scientists than those making a different choice, the so-called 'halo effect', but that tendency is not strong. Overwhelmingly, most pupils – boys and girls – those choosing science and those not, share the same perceptions. The stereotype of the emotionally reticent male, unworldly, somewhat unsociable, more interested in things than people, holds throughout the student population. So subject choice must involve matching that stereotypical model against one's self-image. Choosing science has different implications for a boy than for a girl.

How close the relationship between personality and attitudes might be is dependent on the example being discussed. For example, an authoritarian personality can be defined as one who possesses a set of authoritarian attitudes, making the personality–attitudes link very close. However, even then, the two dimensions are conceptually different, and neither is redundant. Although we may choose to define an authoritarian personality in terms of the attitudes displayed, personality considerations would raise other questions as well, such as seeking a model for the cluster of attitudes and their development in the person. We might, for example, want to describe the development of the authoritarian personality in terms of childhood experiences.

What emerges from this analysis is that we can well use the results of attitude studies to gain insight into personality factors, but observed attitudes will also be influenced by the context in which they are measured. The attitudes of people to science will be influenced both by their underlying personality and natures and by the experiences which they have had of science from such as science lessons and from the media. With that situation in mind consideration can now be given to personality factors.

Notes and References

1 P.L. Gardner, 'Attitudes to science: a review', *Studies in Science Education* Volume 2 (1975) pages 1–41.

2 For example, L. Hudson, *Frames of Mind*, Methuen (London) 1968 and C.G. Carré and J.O. Head, *Through the Eyes of the Pupil*, McGraw-Hill (UK) (Maidenhead) 1974.

3 L. Hudson, *Frames of Mind*, Methuen (London) 1968.

4 G. Basalla, 'Pop science: the depiction of science in popular culture' in G. Holton and W. Blandfield, *Science and Its Public: The Changing Relationship*, Boston Studies in the Philosophy of Science, Volume 33, Reidel (Dordrecht, Holland) 1976.

5 L. Hudson, *Frames of Mind*, Methuen (London) 1968 pages 35–36.

6 H.J. Butcher, 'An investigation of the "swing from science"', *Research in Education*, Volume 1 (1969) pages 38–57.

7 D. Hutchings, J. Bradley and C. Meredith *Free to Choose*, Oxford University Department of Education 1975.

8 H.J. Butcher, see 6 above.

9 J. Bronowski, *Science and Human Values*, Hutchinson (London) 1961 page 86.

10 K. Keniston, *The Uncommitted*, Harcourt, Brace and World (New York) 1965 pages 62 and 255.

11 C.G. Carré and J.O. Head *Through the Eyes of the Pupil*, McGraw-Hill (UK) (Maidenhead) 1974 page 71.

12 C. Selmes, 'The attitudes of 12/13 year old pupils' *School Science Review* Number 174 (1969) pages 7–14.

13 E.W.M. Potts, 'Dainton and the schools: a school view 2' *Trends in Education*, Volume 11 (1968)

4
The Masculine Pursuit of Science

One immediate problem which arises in writing about the personality characteristics associated with a liking for science is that much of the evidence relates only to males. Both Terman's and Roe's studies, reported in Chapter 1, suffer from that limitation. As the evidence is qualitatively different for the two sexes there are merits in scrutinising it separately for the sexes, which is the tactic followed in this and the next chapter. Fortunately, other advantages emerge from that approach, not least because the lack of women in science has led to specific initiatives to study and remedy that situation.

The links between personality and the pursuit of science among males will be examined under five main headings: emotional reticence, authoritarianism, conservatism, diligence, and finally, socio-economic background.

Emotional Reticence

The belief that scientists have a relatively low interest in people and a corresponding high interest in 'things' in the material world, runs right through the literature. Over a hundred years ago Galton contrasted the sober, intellectual endeavours of the scientist with the life-style of poets and artists, saying of the latter:

They are a sensuous, erotic race, exceedingly irregular in their way of life . . . their talents are usually displayed early in youth, when they are first shaken by the tempestuous passions of love.[1]

The scientist's lack of interest in people has been attributed to isolation in childhood as a consequence of the early loss of parents, being an only child, experiencing a period of prolonged illness, and so forth, so that the child develops an interest in surrounding objects to provide the stimulus which is not coming from other people. Eiduson commented on the forty American scientists which she studied:

This commonality of isolation may not seem significant in itself. What is important, however, is that such experiences invariably led scientists to look to their own resources for solace and amusement. What they did by themselves varied according to age and individual difference . . . Often there was no goal set, no product, no result at the end; they played for play's sake. Some merely spent hours in daydreaming or toyed with ideas and symbols. What they gained was the enjoyment, the intrinsic satisfaction in the activities, and the fun of testing.[2]

The importance of parental loss, particularly in the development of highly creative scientists, has been commonly pointed out, but that may no longer hold true in the twentieth century with our lower mortality rates.[3]

Sometimes the social isolation of the scientists has been seen to be verging on the abnormal, for example, Watson writing about British scientists in the 1930s suggested:

The scientist may withdraw from his fellow-men by going into actual physical solitude, or by cultivating the internal solitude of the man who has the power of being 'alone in the midst of the crowd'. *Such an exceptional self-sufficiency will not be found except in an abnormal cast of mind.* [His italics][4]

Similarly Kubie on the basis of his clinical experiences said that:

. . . The emotional problems which arise early in the careers of young scientists are more taxing than those which occur in other careers . . . The young scientist often reaches maturity after a lopsided early development . . . A typical history is that an intellectually gifted child develops neurotic tendencies which hamper his early aggressive and psychosexual development . . . If success rewards his consolatory scholarly efforts during adolescence, he may in later years tend to cultivate intellectual activity exclusively. In this way absorption in the intellectual life will frequently be paralleled by an increasing withdrawal from athletic and social and psychosexual activities.[5]

Possibly Watson was too influenced by the prevailing psychoanalytical explanation for creativity, and Kubie was too influenced by his interest in maladjustment and disorder, to make

41

balanced judgements. At first sight there is little evidence to make quite such a strong argument. For example, as noted earlier, personality tests with student populations show that scientists are generally stable, with low scores on a neuroticism scale, although these findings can be questioned. It has long been recognised by psychiatrists that some people tend to exaggerate their neurotic traits, the so-called 'sensitizers', while in contrast others, the 'repressors', will tend to deny them. One cannot, therefore, simply take psychometric test results at face value. In this context the findings of Hudson,[6] are particularly pertinent. He showed that convergers, who were generally the science specialists, gave vastly different responses to open-ended questions depending whether they were answering as themselves, or in some assumed role. Under the latter conditions some particularly sadistic, aggressive or sexually explicit responses were gained from persons who normally projected a quiet, controlled image.

Similar findings were noticed by the present author in using sentence completion tests with adolescent populations. Often the boys who expressed the wish to specialise in science, initially maintained a carefully controlled image which later might be dropped so that an intensity of feeling would be revealed. For example, the sentence stem 'When a child will not join in group activities . . .' drew from most girls, and the boys not choosing science, sympathetic and sensitive responses such as 'he should be encouraged, but not forced to join in.' Among the boys opting for science about half gave hostile or callous responses, e.g. 'he is stupid', 'he is selfish' and 'he deserves to be unpopular'.

Similarly the sentence stem 'Crime and delinquency could be halted if . . .' drew unsympathetic responses from the boy scientists, e.g. 'all criminals were castrated' or 'after being in prison ten times all criminals were hung'. This mix of emotional reticence, combined with a tough, rather unfeeling attitude to others, was characteristic of the boy scientists among the population being studied.

McClelland, in reviewing responses to some clinical tests, made the comment that 'scientists react emotionally to human emotions and try to avoid them'.[7] That suggestion lends support to the view that much of the appeal of science lies in its apparent emotional neutrality, and a scientist may feel threatened if forced

42

to be involved in emotionally explicit situations. In that event one might anticipate that the emotional initiatives within a marriage lie with the wife. Eiduson confirmed this view:

... the interviews reveal that the scientists are not able to give the most significant part of themselves to home and family ... As a result, their wives and children know those aspects that encompass the commonplace and pragmatic, but they know very little of those aspects of the scientists' personality that are concerned with the personal and the intimate ... Since their work demands a kind of intellectual functioning that is free from conflict, and from pressing emotional demands at home, the men depend on their wives to facilitate this.[8]

A more recent study of the wives of the Apollo scientists emphasised their key role in maintaining the emotional equilibrium:

... science, both as a characteristic method of obtaining knowledge and as a characteristic body of knowledge, has not only emphasised but glorified disinterested objectivity ... What has not been so readily appreciated is that ... it has extracted a social cost from its silent partners ... science is deeply dependent upon women for the care and management of its affective or emotional life.[9]

Authoritarianism

The idea of the authoritarian personality goes back to the famous study of anti-Semitism in the United States by Adorno et al.[10] which made two points. The first is that a series of attitudes tend to cluster together, these being a rigidity in thinking, a distrust of uncertainty and ambiguity, a willingness to accept rules, structures and authority and an intolerance of people who are 'different' such as those from other racial, religious or social groups. Secondly, it was argued that this clustering of attitudes was not coincidental, that they were all manifestations of a personality type, which in turn was generated by earlier experiences of the individual concerned.

The Adorno study attracted criticism as it associated authoritarianism with right wing politics, a reflection of its original focus, nevertheless much of the work still commands respect and it has inspired further study, for example on dogmatism and open and closed attitudes of mind.

Remembering that science is often described in terms of its power to provide order to our perceptions of the universe, to seek patterns in place of confusion and to give explanations to our observations, its appeal to those who are most uneasy about coping with uncertainty and ambiguity can be appreciated.

Much of the evidence associating authoritarianism with science comes from studies of student populations. One survey of undergraduates found that scientists were markedly less tolerant of ambiguity and uncertainty and displayed the most prejudice against racial and other minorities, while another study showed that science students demonstrated the least interest in work which was adventurous and which broke away from expected, conventional routines.[11]

The authoritarian traits can also be expressed by the extent to which a student is syllabus-bound. Such a student will require the syllabus to be clearly laid out and strictly adhered to. In contrast, the more syllabus-free student welcomes opportunities to explore peripheral issues which catch the attention, and tolerates the lecturer who likewise makes an interesting digression. Entwistle and Wilson found the most syllabus-bound students in the departments of chemistry, mathematics, engineering and French.[12] These differences seem well established before students reach higher education, for Hudson reported that with 16 year old boys convergers tended to be more syllabus-bound than divergers, by a ratio of 3 to 1, and in turn, the convergers tended to be the science specialists.[13]

Science might appeal to an authoritarian person not only for its innate quality, the search for pattern and order, but also for the way science research is organised and structured. Many writers on the sociology of science have described just how tight a social system dominates science research; with the individual having to work as a member of a team, needing access to expensive equipment, wanting recognition from the accepted journals and authorities, and to gain these facilities having to conform to the implicit rules of the scientific community. A worker in the humanities might face difficulties in getting unorthodox ideas published in the conventional journals but would be unlikely to require access to laboratory facilities to pursue work and consequently would be able to enjoy a greater measure of independence.

44

Conservatism

The evidence for widespread conservatism among scientists, at least in the recent past, comes from various sources. For example *The Times Higher Education Supplement* made surveys of the voting intentions of academics in the two general elections in 1974 and both surveys showed scientists as more right wing than their colleagues in the humanities and social sciences. Fisch[14] listed a number of American studies coming to a similar conclusion. There seems also to be general agreement that within the sciences, those on the applied side, particularly engineers, are the most conservative. Although these studies were principally concerned with political attitudes, this conservatism seems to extend into the totality of life-style and beliefs.

Payne and Bird looked at students in British polytechnics and drew attention to the irony that although these institutions were largely a product of a Labour government, conceived as a radical alternative to the traditional universities, they were, in fact, dominated by the 'working class Tory code of the engineers'.[15] Entwistle and Wilson found the most radical university undergraduates in sociology and the most conservative in engineering, chemistry and physics.[16]

This conservatism may come as a surprise, for scientists are frequently represented as the iconoclastic harbingers of the brave new world, the men, to quote Snow, having 'the future in their bones'. In his novels and his essays Snow contrasted the radicalism of scientists in the 1930s with the more recent position. Obviously he was writing impressionalistically, and may have been too strongly influenced by the role of a few charismatic radical scientists in the 1930s, such as Einstein and Bernal, but there does seem to be some evidence to support his view. For example, Werskey has written[17] on the influence of the radical 'visible college' among British scientists in the 1930s, telling of the work of Bernal, Hogben, Needham, Levy and Haldane. Jenkins[18] describes the struggle of this group to capture the 'hearts and minds' of their fellow scientists in the 1930s, although with some opposition from colleagues such as Julian Huxley.

Assuming that there was a change between the 1930s and 1970s we might ponder its cause and significance. One factor since the last war has been the incorporation of scientists into the centres of power, for example as government advisors. No longer are they the critics at the door challenging the arts-dominated and educated establishment. They are now the unacknowledged legislators themselves. This increase in responsibility has been accompanied by a new demand for loyalty, as demonstrated by the Oppenheimer affair in the United States. No one accused Oppenheimer of an act of commission, or that he had betrayed secrets or sabotaged work, merely that he was guilty of an act of omission, by failing to display sufficient enthusiasm for the hydrogen bomb project. The role of the scientist as critic was clearly threatened. More recently Easlea has written a detailed account of the links between science, politics and control of finance and allied resources in Western societies.[19]

Another factor underlying the apparent change in the decades following the 1930s might lie in a changing concept of left and right in politics. In the 1930s the Left was usually identified with the model of Soviet Russia. Such a Left might have appealed to scientists, for Marxists, from Engels on, have put a high value on science. In recent years with the widespread disillusionment with Russia, some of the most active left wing groups have had anarchist undertones, with a deep distrust of all powerful governments and organisations. This New Left has less obvious affinity to science and its methods.

Rose and Rose[20] detected a further change occuring in the 1970s possibly as a consequence and reaction to the Vietnam war: the community of scientists was again becoming more politicised and radical, a movement currently manifest in the revival of nuclear disarmament groups and the strength of environmental protection groups. It is too early to judge how deep and fundamental is this change. Among contemporary students the social scientists still seem to be the most radical and the physical scientists and engineers the least.

Diligence

The fourth reported characteristic of male scientists is their apparent diligence, a willingness to work hard and pay little attention to social life, entertainment and amusements. Such description has a puritan tone and scientists have been described in terms of conforming to the Protestant work ethic.

Certainly the association between Protestantism, capitalism and the rise of modern technological societies has been extensively discussed. Weber[21] attributed the shift of wealth and trade after the Reformation from the Mediterranean countries to Northern Europe directly to the effects of Protestantism on the population. Sloth became a much greater sin than covetousness. The self-made newly rich were held up as a model of industry and enterprise, rather than as a threat to the existing social order. The argument goes that under those conditions society generated the entrepreneurs capable of financing new industries and an adaptable, mobile labour force. This argument can be extended to explain the rapid economic growth of North America compared with the failure of the Latin American countries to realise their economic potential. Even if one accepts this general thesis, however, it is difficult to assess the relative contribution to economic development. To what extent was Britain's early industrialisation due to the social mobility and enterprise of its peoples, and to what extent to natural resources? Britain had ample supplies of water, coal, iron, tin and copper ores (only a century ago Britain was the world's biggest producer of the latter two metals) and was geographically well situated for trade.

Merton showed that in its early days the Royal Society had a disproportionate number of Puritans in its ranks and furthermore that there was a close intellectual link:

... certain elements of the Protestant ethic had pervaded the realm of scientific endeavour and left their indelible stamp upon the attitudes of scientists towards their work. Discussions of the why and wherefore of science bore a point-to-point correlation with the Puritan teachings on the same subject.[22]

This willingness to work very hard has been noted in most surveys of scientists, not just those of the successful and creative, so possibly the experience of science students with the long hours demanded for laboratory work acts both as a training and screening procedure.

However, Zinberg[23] in a study of chemistry undergraduates at one London University college has shed some doubt on this belief that scientists conform to such an ethic. She found that the students rejected the traditional values associated with science, which were still held by their tutors, and, in fact, actually envied arts students. She suggested that this feeling of alienation from the stereotypical scientists was likely to generate apathy, and tutors needed to recognise that with the increase in recruitment into the sciences in the last few decades there may well have been a qualitative change in the intake.

A check was made on this possibility by the present author using a questionnaire with sixth formers. With four items:

(a) I rarely tell lies,
(b) I am usually punctual for a meeting or appointment,
(c) I believe that it is worth working hard at school to get a better job later on,
(d) I am a quiet and serious person,

the male scientists tended to score in conformity to the ethic. But with items in a second cluster the reverse was true. These were:

(e) I enjoy parties and discotheques,
(f) I enjoy wearing fashionable clothes,
(g) I tend to spend money as soon as I get it.

Caution is needed in attempting to interpret the results from just one survey, but it appears that the whole construct of conforming to the Protestant ethic needs re-examination. Male science students evidently believed themselves to possess the virtues listed in the first cluster of items, but were simultaneously, as Zinberg suggested, strongly interested in enjoying a rich social life.

Socio-economic Background

There has been an accumulation of evidence indicating that science students tend to come from lower class socio-economic backgrounds than students in other areas. One study of about 8 000 students graduating in 1960 showed that the 2 690 male scientists in the group clearly came from lower status schools and universities[24] while another study found the students in a technological university came predominantly from working class homes.[25] It is not clear to what extent this bias in the social background of scientists is a particularly British phenomenon. The evidence from the United States does not reveal a similar effect there.

In an explanation of the British evidence Box and Ford[26] suggested that science might provide a convenient solution to student marginality, in which a student from a working class background might well experience considerable difficulties in adjusting to the predominantly middle class norms and procedures of a university. Science offers a relatively culture-free environment in which to develop. As noted previously the social, political and religious background of a student is likely to have a more direct effect on beliefs and work within history, literary criticism or sociology, than in the pure sciences.

The more obvious vocational advantages of a science degree might also influence both students and their parents from a working class home in selecting the subject for higher education. Also, the Victorian rejection of trade and technology, with a belief in a liberal education as a training for mind and character, might still prevail in some parts of the independent school system.

Limitations to these Descriptions

Reference was made in Chapter 1 to the quality of psychological evidence relating personality characteristics to a commitment to science. In considering the information provided in this chapter the obvious limitations should be noted.

Nearly all the evidence comes from English-speaking countries, notably Britain, North America and Australia, in the past three decades. In so far as we are concerned with the response of individuals to their experience of the world in general, and to science in particular, the cultural context will affect that response. It is likely that in Victorian England when very different perceptions were held about science and science education from today, the psychodynamics of subject choice were different, so links between personality and subject choice would also be different. Similarly, it is not clear whether the descriptions given in this chapter would hold good in developing countries, or in Russia, where the political, economic and educational systems are so different.

Do the descriptions given in this chapter hold equally for scientists drawn from the different disciplines? Although there has been little direct study of this issue[27] a pattern emerges from the evidence. Physical scientists and engineers seem to conform more closely to the stereotype than biological scientists. Within biology there are probably those working within a physical science paradigm, for example in molecular biology who will be similar to physical scientists, and others working in ecology who may well be more akin to anthropologists and social scientists. That possibility, though, needs empirical verification.

Finally, it must be agreed that what we are describing is just a generalised tendency. Many scientists possess some of these characteristics but not all do. Those who possess these named characteristics do so to varying extents. The closest we can reasonably come to attaching values is to say that *if* scientists err in their behaviour, they are more likely to do so in the direction indicated by these descriptions. The most useful information comes not from simply attaching values to these descriptions, but from considering why scientists might possess these characteristics, and what effect these might have on the way they operate.

Notes and References

1 F. Galton *Hereditary Genius: An Inquiry into its Laws and Consequences*, Macmillan (London) 1869 page 278.
2 B.T. Eiduson *Scientists: Their Psychological World*, Basic Books (New York) 1962 page 50.
3 The case was argued, for example, by S.M. Silverman 'Parental loss and scientists', *Science Studies* Volume 4 (1974) pages 259–264. Hooke, Newton, Rumford, Berzelius and Eddington all lost their father before their tenth birthday while Pascal, Boyle, Huyghens, Cavendish, Priestly, Lavoisier, Kelvin and Clarke Maxwell lost their mother before that age. The suggestion that such considerations may not operate today comes from W.R. Woodward 'Scientific genius and loss of a parent', *Science Studies* Volume 4 (1974) pages 265–277.
4 D.L. Watson, *Scientists are Human*, Watts (London) 1938. This book is not easy to locate these days but it is worth reading, being well ahead of its time and anticipating many of the research findings reported here.

5 L.S. Kubie 'Some unsolved problems of the scientific career' *American Scientist*, Volume 42 (1954) pages 104–112.

6 L. Hudson *Frames of Mind* Methuen (London) 1968 Chapter 7.

7 D.C. McClelland 'On the psychodynamics of creative physical scientists' in H.E. Gruber, G. Terrell and M. Wertheimer *Contemporary Approaches to Creative Thinking*, Atherton Press (New York) 1962 page 149.

8 B.T. Eiduson *Scientists: Their Psychological World* Basic Books (New York) 1962 pages 203–204 and 209.

9 I. Mitroff, T. Jacob and E.T. Moore 'On the shoulders of the spouses of scientists', *Social Studies of Science* Volume 7 (1977) pages 303–327. That title was inspired, of course, by Newton's comment 'If I have seen farther, it is because I have stood on the shoulders of giants.' The study itself was of a group of physicists and some of the Apollo scientists.

10 T.W. Adorno *et al. The Authoritarian Personality*, Harper and Row (New York) 1950.

11 M. Oxtoby and B.M. Smith 'Students entering Sussex and Essex Universities in 1966: some similarities and differences, 2, *Research in Education*, Volume 3 (1970) pages 87–100 and D. Child and A. Smithers, 'Some cognitive and affective factors in subject choice' *Research in Education* Volume 5 (1971) pages 1–9.

12 N.J. Entwistle and J.D. Wilson *Degrees of Excellence: The Academic Achievement Game*, Hodder and Stoughton (London) 1977.

13 L. Hudson *Frames of Mind* Methuen (London) 1968.

14 R. Fisch 'Psychology of science' in I. Spiegel-Rosing and D.de S. Price *Science, Techology and Society: A Cross Disciplinary Perspective*, Sage (London) 1977.

15 G. Payne and P. Bird 'What are their scientists like?' *New Society* Number 369 (1969) pages 641–643.

16 N.J. Entwistle and J.D. Wilson see 12 above.

17 G. Werskey *The Visible College: A Collective Biography of British Scientists and Socialists in the Thirties*, Allen Lane (London) 1979.

18 E.W. Jenkins, *From Armstrong to Nuffield*, Murray (London) 1979. Events such as the Spanish civil war clearly polarised people in the 1930s, and writers, such as Auden and Spender, were like scientists to the left of the political spectrum. Many literary figures, however, including Eliot, Wyndham Lewis, Ezra Pound and Yeats were closer to the other pole, so that overall the literary world emerged with less consensus than the scientists.

19 B. Easlea *Liberation and the Aims of Science*, Chatto and Windus (London) 1974.

20 H. Rose and S. Rose *The Radicalisation of Science*, Macmillan (London) 1976.

21 M. Weber *The Protestant Ethic and the Spirit of Capitalism*, Unwin (London) 1930. It was first published in German in 1904–5 in *Archiv für Sozialwissenschaft und Socialpolitik* Volumes 20 and 21.

22 R.K. Merton 'Puritanism, pietism and science' in B. Barber and W. Hirsch *The Sociology of Science*, the Free Press of Glencoe (New York) 1962 page 35.

23 D. Zinberg 'The widening gap: attitudes of first-year students and staff towards chemistry, science careers and commitments' *Science Studies*, Volume 1 (1971) pages 287–313.

24 R.K. Kelsall, A. Kuhn and A. Poole 'The young science graduate' *Universities Quarterly* (1971) pages 353–368.

25 D. Child 'A comparative study of personality, intelligence and social class in a technological university' *British Journal of Educational Psychology* Volume 39 (1969) pages 40–46.

26 S. Box and J. Ford 'Commitment to science: a solution to student marginality?' *Sociology* Volume 1 (1967) pages 225–238.

27 About the only study is by J. Collings and A. Smithers 'Psychological profiles of physical and biological choosers' *Research in Science and Technological Education* Volume 1 (1983) pages 5–15. They studied nearly 2000 sixth form students, the findings revealed strong sex differences as well as the expected differences between physical and biological scientists.

5

Women in Science

The lack of women in science is not new, although awareness of it has markedly increased in recent years. Women have long been poorly represented in higher education and the professions but whereas with many careers, such as law, there has been a shift in the past two or three decades, the physical sciences and engineering have remained strikingly male-dominated. The growing power of the feminist movement, the recognition that so many important careers are science-based, and the 1975 Equal Opportunities legislation have all highlighted this discrepancy. In turn this has led to intervention initiatives such as those by some Local Education Authorities asking schools to consider their policies and procedures with respect to equal opportunities, with the setting up of several research groups,[1] and with a rapidly expanding literature.[2] Unfortunately it is not that easy to make sense of the mass of evidence being quoted, much of it being more useful in challenging existing ideas than in suggesting anything new.

The Proportion of Women in Science

There is no difficulty in demonstrating the paucity of women in science and engineering. The effect is manifest by the 16+ level and continues, with ever increasing inbalance, from then on. Tables 5.1 and 5.2 show the proportion of women, to the nearest percentage point, passing GCE A levels and in first year university undergraduate courses in 1979.

The proportion of women entering the physical sciences and engineering has not changed dramatically in recent years despite efforts to remedy the shortfall.

**Table 5.1 Percentage of females
among successful A level
candidates**

All subjects	44
English literature	70
French	66
Biology	53
History	50
Geography	41
Chemistry	31
Mathematics	25
Physics	19
Technical drawing	2

Source: DES Statistics of
         Education, 1979, Volume 2.
         HMSO, 1981

**Table 5.2 Percentage of
females among
university undergraduates**

All subjects	39
French	81
English	67
History	49
Geography	44
Law	40
Biological sciences	40
Medicine	39
Mathematics	29
Chemistry	24
Physics	15
Engineering and technology	7

Source: DES Statistics of
         Education, 1979, Volume 6.
         HMSO, 1982

Explanations for the Dearth of Female Scientists

Many explanations for figures as in Tables 5.1 and 5.2 have been
offered but will not usually stand up to close scrutiny.

Perhaps the commonest possibility given in psychological literature is of differences in cognitive abilities, women seen as
inferior to men in mathematical and spatial skills and superior
with verbal tasks. What is the evidence? Maccoby and Jacklin[3] list
35 studies of quantitative factors, of which 16 showed male

superiority, 4 female superiority and the remaining 15 no significant difference between the sexes. For spatial abilities 34 found male superiority, 5 female, and 62 found no difference. With verbal items 15 studies found male superiority, 42 female and 103 found no significant difference. Broadly speaking we can see some support for the common belief in differences in aptitudes but the very large number of inconclusive studies in each case should be noted. How important are these effects? Even when statistically significant differences are found they are usually only of the order of 0.2 standard mean difference (mean of standard deviations). Perhaps a real understanding of that value can be obtained by showing two overlapping normal distribution curves separated by that difference, Fig. 5.1. It can be seen that only at the extreme ends of the ability range are population sizes sufficiently different to give a ratio between the sexes anything like those found in Tables 5.1 and 5.2.

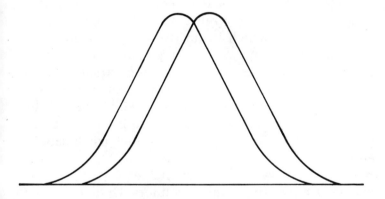

Fig. 5.1 Overlap between two normal distribution curves separated by 0.2 standard mean difference

I have already noted in Chapter 2 the threshold effect with respect to cognitive abilities, and applying that concept to these studies of sex differences suggests that the cognitive differences cannot adequately account for the lack of women scientists. There are enough women in Britain with all the measured cognitive skills to fill every post in science and technology, not merely gain their half share.

There are many further reasons for doubting the importance of small differences in measured performance. Subject and career choice in our society are complex issues involving both a personal psychology and a social context, so that one factor in isolation is unlikely to hold the key. We might note too, despite the reported female inferiority in spatial skills, that women fill a majority of the places in art and design courses. Also one of the few science areas where appreciable numbers of women have worked is in crystallography, which must be one of the disciplines most demanding of spatial ability.

Another argument offered for the lack of women in science has been in terms of institutional factors, in the teaching received in single sex schools, in the attitudes of university admission tutors, and so on. It might have been plausible at the time when a high proportion of entrants to higher education came from single sex grammar and independent schools to argue that girls were disadvantaged in terms of the teaching they received in the physical sciences. A vicious circle could have been set up, the lack of female science graduates being reflected in less science being taught in girls' schools, which in turn would affect university entrance. In that event we would expect girls to benefit from the increase in coeducation so they would now compete more successfully for places in higher education. That conclusion has not been supported by the data on university entrance and Ormerod[4] has demonstrated that fewer girls opt for science in coeducational schools than in girls' schools. It appears that coeducational schools reinforce the stereotypical sex roles.

It is not, of course, easy to estimate whether any informal sex bias exists among university admission tutors. Until 1975 some medical schools operated a quota system, with females being kept to, say, 25 per cent, but such formal arrangements no longer exist. In the last decade the physical science departments of many universities and polytechnics have been desperately short of suitable candidates coming from schools and it would seem unlikely that any appropriately qualified candidate would fail to gain a place in a physical science department.

Clearly demographic factors are important. In times of war women have successfully run factory production lines, driven trucks and laboured on farms, only to be replaced when the men returned. The high proportion of women in medicine in Russia seems to be a reflection of the sex inbalance after the last war and more recently there have been signs of the female dominance being reduced. In most countries women's careers have tended to gain low status, for example teaching and nursing in this country and again medicine in Russia. Once the sex balance changes, as is currently occurring with much office employment in Britain, the job status changes too, to adjust to the new labour force. Male dominance of high status professions adds a further barrier to women entering many science based careers.

Characteristics of Women who Choose Science

Another line of enquiry is to ask what, if any, are the specific characteristics of the minority of females who opt for science in their education and careers.

One widely reported characteristic for women science students is that they are highly extraverted. 'Could it be', asks Child 'as Eysenck's researches suggest, that the extravert, being less susceptible to social conditioning, is in consequence less concerned about what others might think irregular or unfeminine career choices?'[5] A study of 500 sixth form girls by Stamp[6] would support that suggestion. She found that girls specialising in mathematics were more reserved, stable, tough-minded and radical than those specialising in French. That cluster of characteristics hints at the determination necessary to choose a subject against the sex stereotype.

Perhaps the most detailed study of female science students came from Smithers and Collins who looked at 1897 sixth form students including 254 female scientists.[7] They set out to test three hypotheses about the girls specialising in science: that they would be a distinctive group, that they would be aware of the masculine image of science, and that they would tend to come from single sex schools.

Taking those propositions in reverse order, we find only limited support for the hypothesis relating to the schools. More girls from single sex schools opted for science but that effect was only appreciable among the less able pupils. The second hypothesis was confirmed. Boys and girls had similar stereotypical images of scientists and agreed that science students, of either sex, tended to be masculine in character. With respect to the first hypothesis, the evidence is that female sixth form scientists were a distinctive group, characterised by their negative view of their own social attractiveness. They saw themselves as being less feminine, attractive, sociable and popular than the other girls rated themselves. It should be noted, however, that studies of undergraduate female scientists have not detected this negative self-image.[8]

Alison Kelly points out that crucial subject choices tend to be made when pupils are moving into early adolescence and are most conscious of their sex roles.

Science, particularly practical science, is perceived as masculine, by pupils, both male and female, science specialists and non-scientists. It may be this masculine image which deters girls from enrolling in science courses. Around the age of puberty, when they are making their subject choices, girls are often very concerned with establishing their femininity. So they avoid becoming involved in anything which has masculine connotations – and this includes science. Girls are reluctant to compete with boys in traditionally masculine pursuits such as science, for fear that if they do so they will appear less feminine. The well-established fact that more girls enrol in science courses in single sex schools than in coeducational schools (DES 1975) can be attributed to the lesser importance of sex roles in schools where only one sex is present.[9]

It might follow from her comment that if subject choice were delayed until a girl had achieved a firmer self-identity in later adolescence then she would find it easier to opt for science if she wanted to.

The only other way to make science more attractive to girls might be to erode the male image attached to it, but that appears deep-rooted in our culture. We can try to reduce sexism in science textbooks but Jan Harding reminds us that a sexist bias can be discerned even in a recent series of books dealing with the social aspects of science, that is the Association for Science Education series *Science in Society* published in 1981.[10]

We know from classroom observation studies that teachers, both male and female, tend to give more attention to boys in science lessons. Girls tend to be dismissed with bland words of encouragement while boys receive more detailed criticism. That difference in treatment would again handicap the girls.

There is also evidence that the few women who do achieve fame within the scientific community suffer from unhelpful and grudging acceptance, as shown by the reluctance displayed by many, such as Ramsay, to give full credit to Marie Curie for her pioneering work, and more recently with Rosalind Franklin and the discovery of the DNA double helix structure. Since the publication of Watson's story of that discovery, Franklin's role and contribution has been the subject of considerable debate.[11]

Certainly she was initially underestimated. Her X-ray photographs of DNA supplied the parameters of the double helix, she identified the two separate forms of DNA, she demonstrated by the Patterson superposition method that the sugar-phosphate chains had to be on the outside of the helix, and she made the accurate measurement of the water content of DNA. Yet Braggs' introduction to the Watson account pays tribute to the X-ray work of Wilkins, who achieved none of these discoveries, but failed to mention Franklin at all.

Watson himself, despite a generous tribute in the epilogue to his book, conveyed an unfavourable image of Franklin through a series of comments on her appearance and manner:

... it was easy to imagine her the product of an unsatisfied mother ... Rosy had to go or be put in her place ... the best place for a feminist was in another person's lab ... I wondered how she would look if she took off her glasses and did something with her hair ... her dresses showed all the imagination of English blue-stocking adolescents ...

and so forth. By writing of Rosalind Franklin in such terms Watson tended to avoid any meaningful assessment of her as a colleague with whom one might enjoy an open and equal dialogue.

The Psychology of Sex Differences

So far in this chapter a variety of different explanations for the lack of women scientists have been examined, the explanations ranging from differences in cognitive abilities, demographic factors, differences in educational experience, and so forth. That list gives a fair picture of the range of current thinking. Clearly the simple listing of such a variety possible factors is unsatisfactory, even if the different possibilities are not logically contradictory, one would like to know the relative importance of each. Furthermore the lack of a model makes it difficult to ensure that any intervention programme will prove effective, for example if all the crucial events occur in early childhood then intervention programmes aimed at secondary schools will have little benefit for the current generation of students.

As critical choices about subjects are made in adolescence it might prove wise to start by looking at the observed psychological differences between the sexes at that time in life. It is difficult to improve on the summary given by Douvan and Adelson[12] which was based on a study of 3000 American adolescents.

The key terms in the adolescent development for the boy in our culture are the erotic, autonomy (assertiveness, independence, achievement) and identity. For the girl the comparable terms are the erotic, the interpersonal and identity. Differences between the two sets of problems are larger and more complex than the single discrepancy implies; for this discrepancy is so central that it reverberates through the entire complex. For the girl the development of interpersonal ties – the sensitivities, skills, ethics, and values of objects ties – form the core of identity, and it gives expression to much of the developing feminine eroticism . . . For the boy, on the other hand, the integrated capacity for erotic ties and the solution of identity challenge demand separation and autonomy. What the girl achieves through intimate connections with others, the boy must manage by disconnecting, by separating himself and asserting his right to be distinct.

It is not difficult to find evidence confirming the picture given in that passage. Even when overall personality, maturity and cognitive abilities are controlled, i.e. like are compared with like, striking differences were found by the present author in the responses of the two sexes to sentence completion test items. In responding to sentence stems eliciting sources of pride and satisfaction in oneself, the boys stressed personal achievement, often in a competitive context, such as passing an examination, winning a race or a fight. In contrast a significant proportion of girls gave passive responses in terms of receiving praise and compliments from others. However, with sentence stems exploring relationships with parents, the boys often took a self-centred, even exploitive approach, judging a good parent to be one who provided a lot of pocket money and took them to football matches, pop concerts and expensive holidays. Many of the girls showed a mature awareness of the problems and potentialities of the relationship, its changing nature and the reciprocal benefits it gave. We cannot fail to be impressed by the greater sense of autonomy in the boys and the greater understanding of interpersonal relationships displayed by the girls.

How do such differences arise? Perhaps the most important contribution comes from the asymmetric experience children have of parental care, a thesis developed by Nancy Chodorow.[13] In our society most children receive parental care from the mother, or another female acting as a mother substitute. That immediately poses different situations for the two sexes. The young girl is perceived as being almost an extension of her mother, being of the same sex, potentially sharing the same interests and problems. A close relationship often develops which gives the girl the benefit of relating closely to another person, with the sharing of ideas and awareness of another's perspectives. The boy is seen as being different, to be encouraged to achieve autonomy, taking some risks in the rough and tumble of play, learning to keep a stiff upper lip and not display emotion. A higher degree of independence and assertiveness is accepted in the boy.

The consequences of such childhood experiences is that the girl reaches adolescence with a developed sense of interpersonal responsibilities but possibly with a weak sense of personal identity and autonomy. The boy possesses the latter but has paid a price, an inability to handle explicit expression of emotions and some insensitivity to other people's needs.

Hopefully working through adolescence allows the individual to redress the balance so that a clear personal identity and a sensitivity to others are achieved. Nevertheless some work done with young adults by Carol Gilligan[14] suggests that these differences persist into that period of life. They are manifested in making choices, the women attempting to take a holistic view, allowing for all possibilities, the men seeking the simple, direct and best answer to a particular problem.

The model developed here, synthesised from the child studies of Chodorow, the author's own work with adolescents, and Gilligan's findings with young adults, indicates the complex of difficulties confronting a girl opting for science. She not only has to have developed a sense of personal autonomy to allow her to make an unusual subject and career choice but also opts to study a subject which usually places minimal emphasis on the human aspects and applications which girls are likely to be seeking. Furthermore, there has been in recent years another barrier in the assessment system. The increasing emphasis in science on multiple choice and allied methods poses more difficulties for girls whose cognitive style, as described by Gilligan, is to distrust direct answers and display a wish to ponder all the possibilities and consequences. This latter point has considerable educational significance, not least in challenging the concept of 'objective' assessment.

In the light of this description of the development of sex differences what scope is there for teachers to take remedial action to reduce the inbalance? Although the conforming to sex roles is a process beyond the control of science teachers it may still be possible to make changes to what is taught within science lessons so that students' perceptions of science and scientists are in turn changed. Is there such a thing as women's science?[15] The possible implications of that line of argument will be taken up in the final chapter.

Notes and References

1 For example, Girls Into Science and Technology (GIST) at Manchester University, Girls and Science and Technology (GASAT) an international group mainly drawn from Western Europe and North America with its secretariat in Holland, and Girls and Technical Education (GATE) at Chelsea College.

2 This literature is vast and rapidly expanding, perhaps the best starting point is provided by the collection of papers found in A. Kelly *The Missing Half: Girls and Science Education*, Manchester University Press (Manchester) 1981.

3 E.M. Maccoby and C.N. Jacklin *The Psychology of Sex Differences*, Oxford University Press (Oxford) 1975.

4 M.B. Ormerod 'Subject preference and choice in coeducational and single-sex schools' *British Journal of Education Psychology*, Volume 45 (1975) pages 257–267.

5 D. Child 'A comparative study of personality, intelligence and social class in a technological university' *British Journal of Educational Psychology*, Volume 39 (1969) pages 40–46. The words quoted can be found on page 45.

6 P. Stamp 'Girls and mathematics: parental variables' *British Journal of Educational Psychology*, Volume 49 (1979) pages 39–50.

7 A. Smithers and J. Collings 'Girls studying science in the sixth form' in A. Kelly *The Missing Half*, see reference 2 above.

8 I. Lewis 'Some issues arising from an examination of women's exposure to university physics' *European Journal of Science Education* Volume 5 (1983) pages 185–202.

9 A. Kelly 'Sex differences in science enrolments: reasons and remedies' *Collaborative Research Newsletter*, Centre for Educational Sociology, University of Edinburgh (Edinburgh) 1978 page 66.

10 A telling analysis of such bias in these books can be found in J. Harding 'Sex-stereotyping – power and control in the science curriculum' in J.O. Head *Science Education for the Citizen*, The British Council (London) 1982.

11 A strong attack on Watson's account came from a friend of Rosalind Franklin in A. Sayre *Rosalind Franklin and DNA*, Norton (New York) 1975. That book has in turn been criticised as being too one-sided by J. Bernstein *Experiencing Science*, Burnett Books/Andre Deutsch (London) 1979.

12 E. Douvan and J. Adelson *The Adolescent Experience*, Wiley (New York) 1966 pages 347–348.

13 N. Chodorow *The Reproduction of Mothering*, University of California Press (Berkeley) 1978.

14 C. Gilligan *In a Different Voice*, Harvard University Press (Cambridge Mass.) 1982.

15 In a recent letter to me Brian Easlea has spelt out what he envisages a feminine perspective on science might contribute, 'not a masculine power and domination perspective but a feminine understanding and caring . . . to help us become better housekeepers of our world, maintaining the biosphere and its complex interconnections . . .' As one of the most fertile thinkers about science Brian Easlea might be expected to develop his idea in the near future.

6

Commitment and Consequence

We have seen in the last three chapters that the response of individuals to science is strongly coloured by their own personality, which will be a major determinant of career and subject choice. One consequence is that a self-perpetuating cycle is set up, so that the image and experience of science acts as a filter for recruitment to the science based professions, and the people passing through such a filter tend to perpetuate the image.

However, we need to distinguish between highly creative scientists, the more run-of-the-mill professional scientists and science students. Fortunately much the same features emerge in each case, but special consideration of the highly creative will be given later in the chapter.

Subject Choice as a Personal Commitment

Perhaps the first point which needs to be made is that the concept of choice in this context has been shown to be valid. The idea of predestination through the limitations of genetic endowment, particularly with respect to cognitive abilities, is rejected, for while it may be true that not everyone in the population can study science at a specified level the evidence is clear that most people are operating well inside the threshold of their cognitive endowments. Equally invalid is the sociological idea that choice is a myth developed by a consumer society to divert attention from the underlying realities of that society. Clearly some adolescents will be better informed about career opportunities than others, and the amount of thought put into the making of subject choice will vary, but at the very least they will all know about the range of subject options represented in the school curriculum. What does making such a choice involve? Presumably, a matching of what is known

64

about science, its intellectual demands and its vocational potential with what is known about one's abilities, interests and ambitions. The task is to find a reasonable match between these sets of concerns.

We have seen that two possible hypotheses about this process of choosing can be rejected in the light of the evidence. It might have seemed plausible to attribute different choices to different perceptions of science and scientists, so those choosing science see it as easy and interesting, with those opting otherwise holding different perceptions. As already noted there is overwhelming evidence that all students, boys and girls, those choosing science and those not, share the same set of perceptions: science is seen to be intellectually difficult, male-dominated and demanding in its workload. A second possibility which we have also seen as inadequate is that of simple cognitive matching: those who can, do, those who cannot, do not.

What is left? The area for consideration is that of the personality of the choosers, differences in the affective areas, in values and beliefs, not least about themselves. The association of certain personality characteristics with subject choice, an association too strong to be reasonably dismissed as coincidental, hints at some causal mechanism operating. As the crucial choices are made in adolescence it will likely be in adolescent psychology that such mechanisms can be found.

Science and Personal Meaning

Ideas about adolescence have changed in recent years. In particular, the belief in an inevitable period of storm and stress has had to be dropped as many studies have shown that adolescents do not always display undue signs of stress and conflict. Certainly adolescence presents some characteristic challenges and problems, but then equally so do all other phases of life. What are the particular tasks confronting the adolescent? One necessary and almost universal need is that for the acquisition of a personal identity, an idea associated with the work of Erikson.[1]

To say that adolescents undergo an 'identity crisis' might imply that identity achievement is solely a problem of adolescence, and that it will necessarily involve a period of acute distress. Neither

65

implication is always true. Erikson saw the problem being present throughout the whole life of an individual. Thus a child may experience identity problems when first going to school and adults experience identity problems, for example, on retiring. Furthermore Jacques[2] has suggested that many adults face a crisis at about the age of 35 when they realise that time is running out, that the promise of achievement is not enough, achievement itself is now needed, a realisation which often has a profound effect on people, so that some are spurred to greater efforts, others to give up hope. Erikson accepted all this evidence, but argued that for adolescents the achievement of an ego identity must always be a problem.

The resolution of that problem does not, however, necessarily involve the period of acute distress associated with the word 'crisis'. Essentially ego identity development is a task, and one which most adolescents accomplish without too many traumas. The nature of the task is this. The individual in early adolescence is largely defined in terms of other people. X is the son/daughter of Mr and Mrs Y and attends Z school, so that the social class of X is defined by the social class of Mr and Mrs Y. We may assume, because we know the Z school tends to get all its boys involved in rugby playing, that X (if a boy) will play rugby, and so on. By the end of adolescence, however, the individual X has to make crucial choices about career, about life-style including leisure interests, about friends and lovers, and about ideologies. In early adolescence the child probably holds the same ideological view as the parents. That may not be so for the young adult.

It has been argued[3] that the making of these choices relating to a personal identity involves two processes. The first is that of commitment: individuals have to make a choice and cannot go on indefinitely hedging their bets and changing their mind from hour to hour. The second process is to give full thought to all the factors involved in the decision making, including a recognition of their own limitations and strengths. A firm commitment reached after a full consideration of the relevant issues represents a mature choice, in which a sense of personal identity is achieved.

There are less satisfactory outcomes to adolescence. Some adolescents may try to avoid the discomfort of self-examination by clutching at solutions ready-made by others. The process of active thought is avoided and such a person is said to 'foreclose' on the decision. Commitment reached without adequate thought is likely to be accompanied by a rigidity in thinking, as questioning the decision will open up the areas of doubt and uncertainty which have been avoided in making the foreclosure.

Another possibility is that the adolescent, at least for a while, is somewhat overwhelmed by uncertainties and possibilities, so that there is considerable thought and self-examination but little sense of decision and commitment. That uneasy period, described as a moratorium, can often be observed in adolescents: a period of uncertainty about their own destiny, a concern with all the problems and ideals of the world, a scrutiny of a range of ideologies in search of assistance. The period of moratorium is an uncomfortable one for parents and friends as well as adolescents, and therefore tends to provide motivation to make decisions and thus acquire a personal identity. In contrast, however, such motivation does not exist with the person who has undergone foreclosure, and as noted previously, might resist further consideration of the issues.

These ways of handling the decision making processes of adolescent identity acquisition are summarised in Fig. 6.1. Some

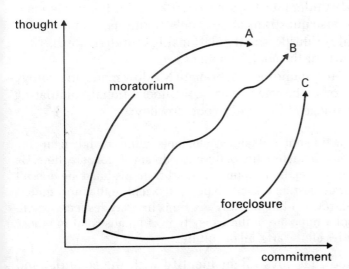

Fig. 6.1 Routes to identity acquisition

adolescents make a fairly even progress towards achieving adult identity (route B), where others experience a period of moratorium (route A). Those who tend to foreclose on difficult issues may later develop a mature identity (route C) but the motivation to do so may not be strong.

How does this description of adolescence relate to subject choice? For girls, the decision to specialise in science almost inevitably involves both considerable thought and firm commitment. It is not an easy choice, as it involves running counter to some of the norms of the peer group in studying a subject associated with boys, so that the girl making that choice must have debated the issues and have some sense of purpose. One might consequently expect those girls who opt for science to be mature and confident in their decision, an expectation borne out by the studies reported in the last chapter.

With boys the situation is more complex. Some will similarly have thought through all the issues and reached a mature decision after due thought. Others, however, will have made the choice by foreclosure. Science with its masculine image and obvious vocational uses is an easy choice for a boy to justify. It does not involve running counter to peer group norms. Above all, its apparently objective, instrumental character can appeal to boys by providing an emotionally undemanding area to work in. Studying science is less likely to raise questions about one's emotions, sexuality, the purpose of life, interpersonal relationships, and so forth, than studying the arts or the social sciences.

The American psychologist Abraham Maslow made an analogy of the perception of the scientist as a cold, unemotional, calculating man with the image of the Hollywood cowboy:

... look at the acting out and fantasy elements in the cowboy figure ... The most obvious characteristics of the boy's dream of glory are there. He is fearless, he is strong, he is 'lone'... Apart from his horse he doesn't love anyone, or at least he doesn't express it except in the most understated, implied, reverse-English way ... He is in every respect imaginable the far, polar opposite of the pansy type of homosexual in whose realm he includes all the arts, all of culture ...[4]

Maslow argued that boys might identify with the scientist and cowboy who appeared to reject overt expression of emotions as being weak and feminine. Furthermore, science provides a more viable alternative than becoming a cowboy as a resolution of adolescent psychosexual conflicts in our society.

Boys opting for science will comprise some who have made a mature choice and others who have foreclosed on science as a mechanism for handling adolescent emotional turbulance. The latter group will tend to be emotionally reticent and resist ideas and changes which threaten their fragile security, a description which matches the empirical evidence.

Perhaps the most significant point to be considered by those involved in science education is how little attraction school science usually has for the large numbers of adolescents, boys and girls, who are experiencing a moratorium. Is this inevitable? In other words, can the image of science as presented to adolescents be changed without losing the essential qualities of science, whatever they may be, in the process? Before looking at these problems within science education in the next chapter, we can consider in a broader context how the mechanisms described influence the working of science.

The Separation of Science

What are the main outcomes for the science community? Not only is science dominated by males, but more importantly, males sharing certain personality characteristics with associated beliefs and values. There are two worrying features of that situation, the lack of communication between the 'two cultures', and a concern that the control of science is solely in the hands of this group of like-minded persons.

In 1959 C.P. Snow gave the famous Rede Lecture drawing attention to the split between the two cultures of the natural sciences and the humanities.[5] He suggested: 'They have a curious distorted image of each other. Their attitudes are so different that, even on the level of emotion, they can't find much common ground.' He urged that knowledge of the Second Law of Thermodynamics, for example, is of such importance that it should become part of our culture, introduced to all pupils in school. There are few signs of change and one suspects that the Second Law is regarded as esoteric as ever. Is such a separation of science inevitable?

It is certainly true that the exponential growth in scientific knowledge this century has made it increasingly difficult for even the professional scientist to keep abreast of developments. It is also true that ultimately any academic study demands a degree of specialisation for its mastery, so any outsider experiences difficulty in grasping all the unique concepts of a topic. Nevertheless as science-related activities play such a crucial role in our society some interest should be shown by everyone and some attempts at exposition made, so a dialogue takes place. It is that lack of communication which Snow lamented.

This seems to have been a particularly acute problem this century, especially in Britain. W.H. Auden wrote:

The true men of action in our time, those who transform the world, are not politicians and statesmen, but the scientists. Unfortunately poetry cannot celebrate them because their deeds are concerned with things, not persons, and are, therefore, speechless.[6]

That sad comment by Auden can be contrasted with the belief in the mid-eighteenth century that science and the arts were partners in uncovering the hidden secrets of the world. Voltaire, who was perhaps the leading savant and literary figure of the century, thought it reasonable to devote more than a decade of his life to experimental science, while men like Benjamin Franklin were conversant with both cultures. Pope's epitaph for Newton summarised the current belief:

> Nature and Nature's laws lay hid in night;
> God said 'Let Newton be!' and all was light.

Distrust about science among literary figures arose with the Romantic writers. Blake, for example, was highly critical of science, not just about the Industrial Revolution giving rise to the 'dark satanic mills' but also about science as a way of thought. He wrote:

> May God us Keep
> From single vision and Newton's sleep

and

I come in self-annihiliation and the Grandeur of Inspiration
To Cast off Bacon, Locke and Newton from Albion,
To cast his filthy garments, and clothe him with Imagination
To cast aside from Poetry, all that is not Inspiration.

It is noteworthy that although Blake was attacking science he nevertheless felt it to be a worthy subject for comment and many other Romantic writers had interests in science and friendships with scientists. Davy was a personal friend of Coleridge and Wordsworth and saw the first edition of their *Lyrical Ballads* through the press. There is still a debate about the extent to which Coleridge anticipated the ideas of evolution and to what extent he was merely repeating ideas he had gleaned from contemporary German philosophers without any real understanding.[7] Shelley took a keen interest in science and Mary Shelley's novel *Frankenstein* reflected the prevailing interest in the early work on current electricity. The two cultures were in active dialogue then.

The real divide between the two cultures came in the latter part of the nineteenth century. The controversy over evolution following the publication of *The Origin of Species* in 1859 divided the academic community so that lifelong friends ceased to speak to each other. In the prevailing mood of positivism scientists tended to react to that controversy by arguing that they were merely reporting objective facts. They said that if those facts were incompatible with religious beliefs then that was unfortunate, but it was not their intention to make comments on religion, merely to pursue the cool, analytical pursuit of scientific truth. A clear division was therefore drawn between scientific enquiry itself and the implications and applications following on from the findings of science. The scientists were disinterested in the applications, merely supplying the factual information.

The most clear articulation of the positivist scientific position came in Ernst Mach's *Die Mechanik* (1883) and Karl Pearson's *The Grammar of Science* (1892). The flavour of the latter work can be assessed from some comments in the opening chapter:

The classification of facts, the recognition of their sequence and relative significance is the function of science . . . Modern science, as training the mind to an exact and impartial analysis of facts, is an education specially fitted to promote sound citizenship . . . it leads us to classifications and systems independent of the individual thinker, to sequences and laws admitting of no play-room for individual fancy . . .

Evidently Pearson had complete confidence in our ability to recognise unchangeable facts, to separate thought from the thinker and knowledge from its social context. With such positivism prevailing within science and in much other thinking of that time, e.g. the belief based on study of the Old Testament that the universe was created in March 4004 BC, the two cultures were not in effective communication.

Our attempts today to regenerate that dialogue will not be easy but scientists can make a contribution. One need is to indicate the true nature of scientific activity with all its human drama. Medawar once suggested that the conventional scientific paper might be regarded as fraudulent in implying objective enquiry and not reporting the true state of mind and intentions of the researcher.[8] Any major scientific endeavour is only likely to be mounted and sustained when the workers have a personal sense of commitment to their work and a belief that they have the key to success. The latter may be hard to justify intellectually at first, as the thinking might run counter to the prevailing orthodoxy. Nevertheless, the strength of the beliefs that individuals, including many eminent scientists, have had in the correctness of their views has led to actual fraud. Examples of manufactured data can be quoted from Mendel to Cyril Burt. Such frauds seem to have been rarely for financial gain or even personal glory, more in the scientists' belief that they knew the answer and the tedious data-gathering stages could be omitted. If such human aspects of scientific endeavour were indicated in textbooks then, although the belief in the correctness of science and scientists might be damaged, it might humanise science and make it appear more relevant and interesting. Such openness, however, would be threatening to those committed to science through foreclosure.

There is an irony in the fact that while in recent years many eminent scientists, like Medawar, have pointed out that science is less objective and value-free than previously realised, workers in other fields, such as geography and psychology, have claimed scientific objectivity for their studies. Such arguments reveal a curiously old-fashioned concept of what science is like.

Clearly there is a need to offer simplified, but one hopes not incorrect, descriptions of science to the public. That process has often been resisted by many professional scientists on the grounds that the ensuing lack of rigour debases science. Possibly Snow's ambition to bring the second law of thermodynamics within the reach of all was unrealistic, but it ought to be feasible to give a sensible introduction to thermodynamics to sixth form science students. If however one looks at the reaction to attempts to do just that with the Nuffield Advanced Level schemes and allied curriculum developments in the late 1960s and early 1970s, one finds a barrage of criticism from some university scientists arguing that anything less than the full, classical treatment of thermodynamics, starting with the Carnot Cycle, is unacceptable. The real task is to provide an introduction to a topic which is within the competence of the learners, but which does not lead to any contradiction or confusion with any more advanced treatment of the topic which might be met later. That task prompts a challenge worthy of the best minds in science.

The Nature of Highly Creative Scientists

So far no distinction has been made between successful, inventive scientists and their less productive peers. Although creativity has attracted considerable attention, the picture that emerges appears confused. One approach has been from a psychoanalytical perspective, which has mainly been concerned with explaining the motivation to toil and persevere. Almost all accounts of creative work testify to the necessity of taking pains for its successful accomplishment. Explanations have been offered in terms of sublimation by Freudians and the fulfilling of a subconscious need to create by Jungians.

In the 1960s there was hope that creativity tests might identify creative potential and lead to a more complete understanding of the development of creative persons. More recently doubts have arisen both about the reliability of such tests, and about their predictive validity.

Biographical studies might prove illuminating, but are vulnerable to distortion. For example Charles Darwin on one occasion described his procedures in these terms:

My first note-book was opened in July 1837. I worked on true Baconian principles, and without any theory collected facts on a wholesale scale, more especially with respect to domesticated productions, by pointed enquiries, by conversation with skillful breeders and gardeners, and by extensive reading.

Such an account certainly did not hold true for Darwin's ideas about coral islands, which he postulated prior to actual observation, and is contradicted by other, later writings, for example: 'As soon as I had become, in the year 1837 or 1838, convinced that species were mutable productions ...'

Almost certainly the latter account was true, that Darwin had become so convinced by 1838 and that for the next twenty years was scrutinising the material for evidence supporting his hypothesis. Without an implicit theory it would be hard to envisage how enquiries might be pointed, reading selected, and attention paid to certain factual evidence. We can only speculate why Darwin attempted to deceive the reader, and perhaps himself, in this fashion, possibly he felt more able to handle the controversy attracted by his work by claiming an objective stance, denying any wish to challenge beliefs by anything more than value-free factual evidence. A more contemporary and acceptable view of scientific discovery is provided by Medawar in which it is agreed that imagination and intuition play a crucial part from the outset.[9]

What sense can be made from the confusion in the literature? Perhaps five main points can be made.

Successful creative workers do not necessarily show early promise in conventional education. Biographical evidence shows this to be true of the truly exceptional scientists, for example neither Darwin nor Einstein achieved much success in their education, and there is evidence that with contemporary successful scientists their early academic career was often undistinguished.

The starting point for ultimate success comes in the identification of the problem or issue needing resolution. Just why a particular issue, whether it related to astrophysics or animal behaviour, should excite the imagination remains unclear, but such an interest is necessary to provide the stimulus for the work.

The next requirement is that of persistence. Often success comes slowly and failure and criticism have to be faced before eventual success is achieved. Had Paul Ehrlich only had the

74

stamina to examine two or three hundred possible chemotherapeutic agents then salvarsan would not have been discovered at the time, and that aspect of medical knowledge might have been held back by decades. This determination often allows the worker to persevere despite discouraging empirical evidence.[10] It has been this issue of motivation and persistence under discouraging circumstances, with minimal hope of success, which has attracted the attention of the psychoanalytical school of workers.

The vital insight which leads to success often comes suddenly, under unexpected circumstances, and often in its ultimate entirety. For example, Poincaré described his own experience thus:

For fifteen days I strove to prove that there could not be any functions like those I have since called Fuschian functions . . . I left Caen, where I was then living, to go on a geologic excursion . . . We entered an omnibus to go some place or other. At the moment when I put my foot on the step the idea came to me . . . I did not verify the idea; I should not have had the time, as, upon taking my seat in the omnibus, I went on with a conversation already commenced, but I felt a perfect certainty. On my return to Caen, for conscience's sake I verified the result at my leisure.[11]

Many similar incidents, such as Kekulé's dream about the snake biting its tail providing a clue about benzene structure, can be quoted. Once the insight has been acquired, the discoverer usually displays supreme confidence in its value, and, like Poincaré, only bothers to verify the idea at a later date.

What precisely characterises the ability to have this flash of insight? The crucial factor seems to be an ability to reconstruct a problem, or to bring together two bits of information which had previously seemed separate. An explanation can then be related to a psychological description: the ability to break set and to be field-independent. Barron draws attention to a finding which is in accord with this view.[12] He descibes the results of using Welsh Figure Preference Tests in which the subjects are asked to state, without justification for their choice, which they preferred of a number of abstract figures. He found the majority of scientists chose symmetrical, regular shapes but creative scientists, like artists, chose more disordered patterns. This distinguished, he suggested, those scientists who prefer to work in ordered environments and the imaginative few who welcome an apparently disordered situation so they might themselves identify or impose order. The former group see disorder as a threat, the latter as a challenge. The parallel is apparent between this line of argument and that of Kuhn in describing scientists who work within an existing paradigm compared with those seeking to generate new paradigms.

The final requirement is to test the idea by accepted scientific methods. Testing comes from the open publication of both experimental methods and data which can then be checked by other workers in the field. It is this final process which has attracted the attention of many philosophers of science, notably Popper, and provides the hallmark of genuine science.

Science in the Nuclear Age

One particular area of concern in recent years has been that separation of science has led to science being controlled by a relatively small group of like-minded people and it has been argued that this group displays one of the less desirable features of masculinity, that of aggression. In the nuclear age this raises obvious worries. One of the few reported differences between the sexes which stands up to scrutiny is the greater aggressiveness of boys, although there is still debate about the cause, to what extent this reflects child-rearing practices and to what extent it has hormonal origins. Writing from a psychoanalytical perspective, Karl Stern argued a link between male sexuality and science:

Quite independently of sociological and cultural shifts of emphasis, there exists an aspect of life which is forever associated with the masculine principle. Just as in the function of the spermatozoon in its relation to the ovum, man's attitude towards nature is that of attack and penetration. He removes rocks and uproots forests to make space for agriculture. He dams rivers and harnesses the power of water. Chemistry breaks up the compound of molecules and rearranges the position of the atoms. Physics *overcomes* the law of gravity . . . [13]

Stern argued further that within the individual and society we need to maintain 'a precious equilibrium' between masculine and feminine qualities and that our contemporary technological society has over-emphasised the masculine virtues.

It is the possible lack of 'precious equilibrium' in contemporary science that causes concern. For example, Brian Easlea has described how, although he originally attributed the callousness sometimes found with respect to the proliferation of nuclear weapons to the way capitalist economies operate, he later felt that the essential quality came from a male wish to display toughness and strength. He pointed out that although the Los Alamos scientists early in the last war were initially motivated by the wish to develop an atomic bomb before Germany, the project eventually acquired its own momentum, so that after the surrender of Germany activity was actually stepped up and the bomb had to be used as a final demonstration of macho virility.[14]

How much weight one gives to the Easlea line of argument can be debated. He quotes from many science writings to demonstrate the range of sexist and aggressive metaphors employed, arguing that these are indicative of underlying personal values. Certainly it is easy to find references to 'the conquest of materials', of 'man controlling the universe', 'penetration of nature's secrets' and 'getting nature to sit up and beg'.

However, the use of metaphors as indicators of underlying values can raise problems as the following study indicates. Noting the characteristics of scientists already described: most being male, with strong masculine interests, and many having lost their fathers in early life, the American psychologist, David McClelland, developed a Freudian explanation. He suggested that scientists experienced a very strong Oedipal situation in childhood which was powerfully suppressed. The difficulty in handling such a hypothesis, of course, is that it is unsinkable. If scientists do not reveal an Oedipal complex then the argument would go that it is strongly suppressed. As direct reference to a potentially Oedipal situation might stimulate that suppressed complex, one of McClelland's students used a metaphors test as an indirect test.[15] The subjects were asked to choose from a list of metaphors which they thought best described nature, the idea being that scientists might opt for those metaphors which contained concealed maternal images. The results were inconclusive. Scientists tended to choose more images which involved sexual symbolism, but not just feminine images. In fact the most popular choice among scientists was, 'A pillar of strength and virility', a metaphor whose symbolism is far from maternal!

Clearly the arguments of Easlea and McClelland are controversial and alternative interpretations of events can be offered. What might prove common ground is a recognition of the lack of meaningful dialogue between the scientific community and the general public about the benefits and dangers posed by such developments as nuclear power and genetic engineering. Too often scientists argue that they are concerned with pure science and not its applications and that the public, lacking specialist knowledge, cannot make decisions involving the application of science. It is that absence of genuine dialogue which has alarmed such writers as Theodore Roszac[16] and has made it too easy for ill-informed opinion to go unchallenged.

Part of the need is an educational one, but one can identify considerable opposition to attempts to introduce social and applied issues into the school science curriculum; nevertheless, diminishing the barriers between the two cultures remains a vital task.

Notes and references

1 E.H. Erikson, *Childhood and Society*, Norton (New York) 1950 and *Identity, Youth and Crisis*, Faber (London) 1968.
2 E. Jacques, 'Death and the mid-life crisis', *International Journal of Psychoanalysis* Volume 46 (1965) pages 502–514.
3 The thesis was first put forward by J.E. Marcia 'Development and validation of ego-identity status' *Journal of Personality and Social Psychology* Volume 3 (1966) pages 551–558. Marcia's work has become very influential and my own thinking has been strongly influenced by his writing. See J.O. Head 'A model to link personality characteristics to a preference for science' *European Journal of Science Education*, Volume 2 (1980) pages 295–300.
4 A.H. Maslow *The Psychology of Science: A Reconnaissance*, Harper and Row (New York) 1966 page 37.
5 C.P. Snow *The Two Cultures: And A Second Look*, Cambridge University Press (Cambridge) 1965 contains the text of the original Rede lecture given in 1959.
6 W.H. Auden *The Dyer's Hand and Other Essays*, Faber and Faber (London) 1975 page 81.

7 The case for Coleridge possessing a firm understanding of the scientific arguments for evolution has been made by P.B. Medawar *The Hope of Progress*, Methuen (London) 1972. Other writers, e.g. N. Fruman in *Coleridge: The Damaged Archangel*, Allen and Unwin (London) 1972 argue that Coleridge's ideas set out in his *Hints Towards the Formation of a More Comprehensive Theory of Life* were taken with minimal understanding from the German philosophers Schelling and Stiffens. It might be noted that contemporary with Coleridge, Goethe in Germany was similarly synthesising current thinking in science and art.

8 P.B. Medawar 'Is the scientific paper a fraud?' *The Listener* (12 September 1963) pages 377–378.

9 P.B. Medawar *Induction and Intuition in Scientific Thought* Methuen (London) 1969.

10 Evidence for this confidence allowing a scientist to retain his belief in his hypotheses and dismissing contrary evidence as aberrant due to some yet unknown complicating factor is quoted by A. Koestler *The Act of Creation* Hutchinson (London) 1964. In this book Koestler developed his idea of 'bisociative' thinking by creative persons, that is the making of connections between previously unconnected ideas and experiences.

11 H. Poincaré 'Mathematical Creation' in P.E. Vernon *Creativity* Penguin (Harmondsworth) 1970 pages 81–82.

12 F. Barron 'The psychology of imagination' *Scientific American* Volume 187 (1958) pages 21–25.

13 K. Stern *The Flight from Woman*, Allen and Unwin (London) 1966 page 23.

14 B. Easlea *Fathering the Unthinkable: Masculinity, Scientists and the Nuclear Arms Race*, Pluto Press (London) 1983.

15 D.C. McClelland 'On the psychodynamics of creative physical scientists' in H.E. Gruber, G. Terrell and M. Wertheimer *Contemporary Approaches to Creative Thinking*, Atherton (New York) 1962.

16 He has written extensively on this topic, perhaps the best starting point is his first book: T. Roszac *The Making of a Counter Culture*, Faber (London) 1970.

7

The Implications for Science Education

As we have seen, the response of individuals to their experience of science is influenced by a variety of factors, ranging from the attitudes and values held by society about men and women, and science and technology, to the psychology of the individual, in turn strongly influenced by personal life experiences. Formal education is only one of many influences and it would be foolish to attribute to the educational system all the faults of the present situation, or all our hopes for the future. Nevertheless there are good reasons for seeing the education system as providing the principal platform for change.

Formal education is the one universal experience. Individuals may or may not know practising scientists personally, they may or may not read science fiction, or watch science based television programmes, or have a hobby involving science. Nearly everyone, however, will experience formal education including some years of science lessons and meeting science teachers. School experiences also occur at times when students are probably forming personal beliefs and values making subject and career choices. Most school science is experienced during adolescence when a sense of personal identity is likely to be acquired.

A further reason for emphasising the importance of the educational system is that it is the part of the complex most open to reform. Even if one wished to see science receive a different presentation in works of fiction, or if one wished to change the values held about sex roles by society at large, it is not easy to suggest how such changes can be implemented in a free society. The educational system has an inertia of its own, as those involved will testify, but nevertheless major changes in school organisation, curricula, classroom practices and educational technology have occurred in the past twenty years or so. There is no reason to doubt that further changes can occur in the next two decades, and that belief lends strength to those wishing to concentrate on the reform of science education.

Within this field our consideration can range from the strategies of the national system and curricula to the tactics of day-by-day classroom practice. Both will be discussed in this chapter but it might be best to start with the wider, general issues, in particular asking what might be wrong with the existing situation.

From the Top Downwards

Our thinking about the curriculum in science has traditionally been dominated by the top end of the educational system. Each stage is seen more as a preparation for the next stage than an educational experience in its own right. The tragedy is that we are always catering for a minority as the majority in a class are likely to terminate their science education at the end of each stage. Consequently we possess university departments and research institutes worthy of world renown but a general population who are not only scientifically illiterate but who often actively dislike science and resist technological innovations. How does this situation come about?

In the golden age of British scientific and technolgical development, the last part of the eighteenth century and the first half of the nineteenth century, the educational establishments played only a minor role in the industrial revolution. Both the universities and the public schools were at a nadir, and much science education took place through apprenticeships, the Mechanics Institutes, and societies such as the Royal Institution and the Birmingham Lunar Society. British science at that time was marked by pragmatism and relevance to technology and everyday life.

After about 1830 science and technology moved into higher education in a number of countries, notably Germany where, for example, Liebig's laboratory at Giessen, established in 1826, spawned whole generations of eminent chemists, including Baeyer, Dewar, Ehrlich, Fischer, Hofmann, Kekulé, Nernst and Van t'Hoff. By the end of the nineteenth century, Germany dominated the world's chemical market. Despite commissions of enquiry the urging of individuals such as Prince Albert, Britain

81

failed to respond in kind. This British failure has been discussed by historians at length[1] and two main contributory factors emerge. Firstly, the possession of the British Empire caused a lot of British risk capital to be invested abroad in the production of raw materials rather than in new manufacturing processes in competition with Germany, France and the United States. The other factor seems to have been the particular social snobbery of Victorian Britain. The entrepreneurs of the industrial revolution were encouraged to enter into the ranks of the gentry, and a key role of public schools was to help the sons of entrepreneurs to grow away from the roots of their fortune. In that social climate anything to do with trade was taboo, and science had to be clearly separated from technology to be acceptable as a subject worthy of study. Hence teaching science was justified for its abstract qualities, training the mind and providing logical exercises that rivalled the classical languages. With that purpose clearly defined, the public schools and universities tentatively allowed science into the curriculum, but British attitudes can be epitomised by the fact that when Oxford University did at last build a chemical laboratory, half a century after Liebig's, it was modelled on the Abbot's kitchen at Glastonbury. Thus Oxford faced the Brave New World!

The low status of Oxford science at that time can be contrasted with Boyle and Hooke working there in the late seventeenth and early eighteenth century. None of the nineteenth century university foundations, other than those which now form Imperial College in London, really followed the model set up in Germany in the 1830s. Although many of the civic universities made initial references to local needs and technologies in their foundation documents and charters, within a few years the concept of learning for its own sake distanced from socially low status technology took over, a process echoed by the developments in many former Colleges of Advanced Technology and Polytechnics within recent years.

There were, of course, exceptions. Within the public school system Armstrong's advocacy of heurism had some influence early this century, but it only survived on a minor scale until the Nuffield schemes were set up in early 1960s. Attempts to produce socially relevant science in schools were discouraged and much interesting work in elementary schools was halted by the provisions of the 1902 Education Act. Half a century later the General Science movement was swamped by the curriculum reforms of the 1960s.[2] Although those schemes succeeded in updating content of courses and introduced ingenious practical exercises they were arguably more intellectually demanding, more dominated by the demand of the universities, than the curricula they replaced. Although in 1962 some of the Nuffield workers did ask about the relevant contribution from psychology[3] most of the schemes were drawn up by brain storming by academic scientists who linked them to the successful school practice of able, experienced teachers drawn from grammar and public schools. Very little attention was given to the simple questions of what boys and girls of, say, 12, 14 and 16 are like, what their abilities and interests might be. One consequence of such thinking was that much of the work was unduly difficult in terms of its cognitive demand.

This argument can be illustrated by an example. In Topic 18 of the original Nuffield O level chemistry scheme there were neat practical exercises relating to reaction rates. These practicals were based on two simple chemical reactions: hydrochloric acid reacting with calcium carbonate, and with sodium thiosulphate solution. The experiments were well chosen, involving simple chemical reactions, were quick and cheap, and presented no undue safety problems. The reactions gave easily observable results such as weight loss, or production of a gas or a precipitate. Unfortunately all the ingenuity in developing such simple and effective practical exercises was jeopardised by the graphical treatments demanded for the data[4]. The students were asked to take the reciprocal of time as the units along one axis, to take slopes from the curves, and so forth. These exercises designed for students of 14, approaching 15, made demands not normally expected even in mathematics lessons, demands which in Piagetian terms involved formal operational thinking. Good chemistry was marred by poor psychology.

Cognitive Matching Strategies

I have already noted that the Piagetian work is under some attack particularly for its theoretical foundations. It might be common knowledge to most teachers that the more complex and abstract ideas in science are very difficult for a high proportion of students to comprehend. Although it may in theory be possible to teach any concept to anyone in a given class, in the real world time and effort might be better employed in selecting content which stretches the students but does not present apparently insurmountable difficulties. That argument is not a plea for deleting all the intellectually challenging content from school science, it is merely questioning whether a particular topic can be simplified without loss of any crucial concepts, or whether more difficult sections can be delayed so the students will bring greater maturity and knowledge to bear.

As reported in Chapter 2, the team responsible for the revision of the Nuffield O level chemistry scheme in the early 1970s found that the mole concept presented considerable difficulties to pupils. What could be done? The mole concept was too central to modern day chemistry thinking to be deleted from the course.

The solution was to split the work on the mole into two parts, so that the concept could be introduced and used early in the course, but a full, rigorous treatment was delayed until the students could cope with the concept more easily. Doubtless similar analysis could be applied with profit to all science curricula so that the learning sequence is not solely governed by the logic of the subject but also by the cognitive demand made by each topic.

Science in Context

Perhaps an even more important need is to present science so that its social and applied context is appreciated. It has already been noted that much conventional school science is unlikely to appeal to adolescents experiencing moratorium, as science rarely seems to address their concern for personal identity and ideals. If appreciation of the utility and relevance of science is achieved in school then it should carry into adult life and help bridge the rift between the two cultures, for those not opting for a science based career as much as anyone else.

Radical change as great as in the early 1960s will be needed in science education, a point appreciated by the Association for Science Education in its discussion paper and policy statements on the secondary school curriculum.[5] In the past, the social and applied aspects of science, if mentioned at all, were presented as an afterthought, a short paragraph at the end of the chapter or a brief discussion at the end of Friday afternoon school. What is needed is to start with the problems and issues with which students can identify themselves and then make use of science to help work towards possible solutions; in other words the teaching pattern would be reversed from much contemporary practice. The adoption of such a curriculum has many implications. It would be foolish to attempt to cover all the same science content and provide the social context within the same time allocation. It is difficult to see how more time within the secondary school curriculum can be given overall to science without a loss of balance, hence the profession will need to accept the prospect of the science content being reduced. One problem within science education has been the attempt to give comprehensive coverage to every subject; in future science teachers may have to follow the example of their colleagues teaching history or literature and aim to draw out general principles from the detailed study of some specific instances.

Adolescents experiencing moratorium, particularly girls, are particularly concerned with humanistic issues, and evidence that biology retains its popularity with adolescents, in contrast to the physical sciences, should cause no surprise. Not only can a more central role for biology be envisaged in a new curriculum but some introduction to psychology and anthropology might be made. Possibly the balance should be that physical sciences take no more than half the time in the school science curriculum with the other half devoted to the biological and humanistic aspects.

Such a new science curriculum introduced into schools would have implications for the functions of the teacher, and in turn for teacher education. It would be necessary to allow students more opportunities to debate issues and to make value judgements relating to science. Such discussions may be familiar to teachers of history or social studies but create additional demands on the science teacher, involving the exercise of new skills and the acceptance of a different relationship with students. The authority vested in a teacher as the person knowing the right answers might be weakened as the new function would involve more the asking of questions and challenging stated beliefs. The compensation should come from science education becoming more lively with greater student involvement.

Making Science Meaningful

Having considered large scale curriculum planning we can now move on to implications for classroom teachers.

One important need is to ensure that the material students experience is meaningful. They arrive at science lessons with an existing cognitive structure, built up from experiences and ideas acquired throughout their whole life. If the ideas they meet within science are compatible with their prior beliefs then learning should be easy. Unfortunately much of science may appear alien, or not relevant to the real world and in that event it will merely be learnt rote fashion, if at all. How can the teacher relate science to the mental world of the learner and make science more meaningful? I will suggest four tactics.

Reformulation

If a student has to explain a concept 'in his own words' then the repetition, parrot-fashion, of rote learnt material will prove inadequate. In order to express the concept in everyday language with familiar metaphors the learner has to relate the newly met concept to the pre-existing cognitive structure, and in so doing meaningful learning occurs. That process is not always easy, as witnessed by the commonly observed hesitations and stumblings experienced by students in explaining a newly learnt concept, yet it is a vitally important process. The obvious managerial problem for the teacher is to find ways of giving all the pupils in a class opportunities to talk and write in this fashion. It would be glib to minimise this problem, but clearly the form in which written work is sought from the members of the class and the nature of discussion within small groups, as during practical work, can determine the opportunities given to individual students for such expression.

Application

Using a newly learnt concept in some novel situation demands that the concept is understood in a meaningful way and has not just been learnt by rote. That conclusion has implications for the type of work which might be set for homework and also provides one justification for doing practical work, a point which will be followed up later.

Making Use of Prior Knowledge

The cognitive structure held by the student prior to a lesson will ensure that new ideas are not approached in a totally naive way, as the learner will tend to have some prior assumptions about the issue under consideration. Once existing and mistaken concepts have been recognised, an appropriate teaching strategy can be developed, for example by producing empirical evidence which contradicts the student's beliefs. As already noted, the obvious reservation about this approach is how one teacher can ascertain and respond to all the different prior beliefs held by all the students being taught. The real need is to listen more carefully to what the students *really* say and to treat their misconceptions as informative rather than just dismissing them as incorrect. It seems that pupils sometimes hold conflicting views for a while: the formal science concepts in school and a folk wisdom in their daily life, a clear example of school learning failing to be fully meaningful.

Involving the Learner in the Teaching Strategy

Too often a student is presented in each lesson with a new topic to 'understand', i.e. incorporate into his/her own pre-existing cognitive structure, without being told exactly why that particular topic is being introduced at that moment. It is left to the learners to identify the rationale behind the learning sequence, and integrate this into their cognitive structure. By any definition that is a high level cognitive process.

If, on the other hand, the learners are told the teacher's strategy and are invited to observe and monitor their own learning, the

87

process should be easier. Currently, hard evidence of the benefits of such teaching is limited but certainly a common complaint among students is that they do not know where the lessons are going, and this sense of purposelessness must be discouraging. Ausubel's 'organisers', statements provide this integrating function and given both at the beginning and end of a topic to sum it up and set it in its context, should help students reorientate their thinking.

The Value of Practical Work

Practical work involves high costs and inconvenience. Laboratories require about twice the floor area of a conventional classroom for the same sized class, they are expensive to equip with the necessary services, capital is needed for the apparatus and ancillary staff are needed to maintain the laboratory. Perhaps it is not surprising that most countries other than Britain have until recently kept school practical work to a minimum and we may need to justify ourselves why we undertake this work.

There have been no recent comprehensive studies in this field but the points raised in the Kerr report (1964)[6] are probably still relevant. Teachers then stressed the motivational role of practical work with younger secondary school pupils and the acquisitions of useful skills for older pupils. What psychological evidence is there for these and similar claims?

Motivation

Most science teachers testify to the positive effects of practical work on pupil motivation yet when I was undertaking a collection of pupils' writings in science[7] I found that a significant minority of pupils expressed a dislike for practical work. This suggests that the situation may not be quite so simple as it seems at first sight. A fuller understanding requires more precise information. Which types of practical work motivates pupils? What about age and sex differences in the response to such work?

Research on personality developments in adolescents reveals that at the age of 12 the majority of pupils are at a very conformist stage while a couple of years later the majority have become much more aware of their own individuality and are more willing to take personal initiatives.[8] It might follow that practical work should be organised in a way that enables the pupils to have increasing opportunity to exercise personal freedom and imagination as they become older. In practice the reverse trend can often be observed. Primary school science lessons often have a fairly loose 'discovery' format but by the middle part of the secondary school the work is tightly structured and limited to a specific law or effect which the practical work is intended to illustrate. We may need to modify the practical exercises given to pupils in the 14 to 16 age range in order to give scope for the exercise of the newly developed sense of personal initiative.

Acquisition of Skills

A common claim for practical work is that it develops useful observational and manipulative skills which can be used later, in employment and higher education. That may well be true, but there is very little solid evidence to prove the point. It has not been demonstrated just what skills are commonly acquired through science lessons, whether science is uniquely effective in such development, and to what extent these skills can be transferred to new situations. School science may be less useful as a preparation for employment than has been commonly assumed, as employers often prefer to retrain workers in their own way and in any event modern instrumentation and automation makes this less important.

A more realistic but vague claim is that practical work gives pupils a 'feel' for a certain type of activity and provides an opportunity to learn whether they like such work and show any aptitude for it. In that case we might argue that all pupils should gain some experience of practical work in order to facilitate career choice.

Enhancing Learning

Perhaps the most convincing case can be made for the claim that understanding practical work enhances the quality of learning. I have already noted that meaningful learning is likely to occur when reformulation is involved and in carrying out practical work the word becomes the deed. Unless instructions are understood, as distinct from being learnt verbally by rote, the student is unlikely to be able to perform the practical tasks. Bruner[9] argued that part of our learning is enactive, occuring through our body experiences. Such learning predominates with very young children but is still useful to adults. How can you teach someone to ride a bicycle or learn to swim other than by getting them to make an attempt to learn from that experience and through the muscles of the body? Verbal instructions are of limited value.

A further gain from practical work is often forgotten. Pupils need to talk to each other about the work and that discussion facilitates understanding. In explaining a point a pupil will need to reformulate the concepts. The less able pupil might understand the explanation from another pupil as it is likely to involve simple vocabulary and commonly understood analogies and metaphors. The role of pupil-to-pupil talk in practical science lessons merits further study.

We might, in concluding this section, note the warning from Novak[10] that practical work is not necessarily a meaningful learning experience. Following on from Ausubel's studies Novak suggests that we need to differentiate between two separate learning parameters: the meaningful-rote continuum and the discovery-reception continuum, which he argues are independent. Some of the claims made for discovery learning in the 1960s and early 1970s tended to suggest that all discovery type exercises must inevitably produce meaningful learning. As we can see from Fig. 7.1 learning exercises like the learning of multiplication tables can be rote and reception, and that well designed practical exercises will involve meaningful discovery learning.

However we can also have meaningful reception learning, for example when a lecturer introduces a new concept which by linking together bits of previously acquired knowledge suddenly makes sense of them. Furthermore poorly considered practical exercises may involve discovery learning but not be meaningful as the learner is doing no more than rather aimlessly trying out a set of 'hit or miss' activities. The crucial message from Novak's work is not to advocate lectures and condemn laboratory work but to suggest that one needs to examine the quality and purpose of these learning experiences more carefully before making judgements.

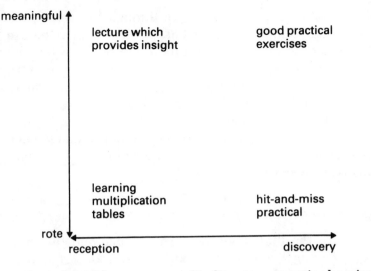

meaningful

lecture which
provides insight

good practical
exercises

learning
multiplication
tables

hit-and-miss
practical

rote

reception

discovery

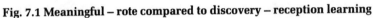

Fig. 7.1 Meaningful – rote compared to discovery – reception learning

Providing Multiple Access to Science

A particular problem is that science often seems to be inaccessible, particularly to someone who failed to master the subject earlier in life. This problem arises largely from the habit of presenting scientific explanations in a linear fashion so that each stage of the argument builds on to what went before. Although this is clearly logical it does present a difficulty to anyone who missed, or failed to understand, the early parts. They might then experience the sense of frustration like that of sprinting to catch a bus, just missing it, and then knowing that how ever hard one runs that bus cannot be overtaken. Accounts of learning tells us that a fair proportion of a new topic will not be understood by a student on one occasion and that there is a need to provide further opportunities for access to the ideas.

Although this point is principally a plea for something like a spiral curriculum in which the key concepts are met several times, albeit in different contexts and at different levels of detail, there are other ways of helping provide this multiple access. A further point, and here science has an advantage over arts subjects, is that different people learn more effectively through the verbal, the visual or through 'hands on' experience. Consequently the use of a wide range of resources and techniques in presentation of a topic should allow access from several directions and also remove the boredom associated with simple repetition of an argument. Informal sources of science education such as the media, home computers and hobbies can also be utilised as means of gaining entry into ways of thinking within science. It is hoped that science will then appear less alien and threatening, and can be brought more into everyday discourse.

The Experience of Science

In dealing with the interaction between science and the individual experiencing it, most of this book has been concerned with one aspect of that interaction. Much has been said about the importance of what the individual brings to that experience, the prior beliefs, attitudes, ambitions and hopes. These will all modify that experience. Very little has been said about the reverse process – how the experience of science might affect the individual – an omission which reflects the lack of firm evidence.

Claims have been made at various times for the value of science education in providing a logical exercise which trains the mind and develops skills which can remain with the learner for life. Such claims may be valid but one might be tempted to treat them with caution because identical claims, couched in much the same language, have also been made at intervals for practically every other subject in the curriculum, from classics to mathematics. There is no clear research evidence for selecting one subject on that basis in preference to others. Nevertheless some tentative psychological arguments can be advanced for the value of science education.

One possibility is that it might help adolescents to 'decentre'. According to many contemporary psychologists, e.g. David Elkind,[11] one of the tasks adolescence involves is moving from a self-centred stance to one where an individual can see another person's perspective, a process necessary for the development of empathy and mature interpersonal relationships. Part of the methodology of science demands the replacement of personal impressions by careful observational measurement and the control of variables. Such experience can bring home the limitations of personal impressions and might generate in the learner a realisation that one individual perspective may not provide the whole picture.

It is possible that it is the quality of the learning experience, rather than the subject content, which is crucial. In the face of such uncertainty the wisest plan must surely be to give each student a balanced curriculum so that the student has access to all benefits the subject may bring, ranging from the opening up of career opportunities to assisting personal development. In such a balanced curriculum science has a key role, because of its vocational importance and because it offers a wide variety of learning experiences in classroom, laboratory and the field. Specialisation involving subject choice should, therefore, be resisted for as long as possible, and we should provide balanced science courses for the whole population up to the age of sixteen, not just boys, not just the able. To do that effectively we need to recognise what these learners are like, their interests and abilities, and to provide an education which not only provides entry to science linked careers for the few, but an interest and appreciation of the strengths and weaknesses of science for the many.

Notes and References

1 For example, M.J. Wiener *English Culture and the Decline of the Industrial Spirit 1850–1890*, Cambridge University Press 1981.
2 For an account of this period within science education see E.W. Jenkins *From Armstrong to Nuffield*, Murray (London) 1979.
3 M. Waring *Social Pressures and Curriculum Innovation: A Study of Nuffield Foundation Science Teaching Project*, Methuen (London) 1979.
4 An illustration of how the use of a computer can overcome the difficulties presented in the data analysis is provided in a companion book in this series: B. Kahn, *Computers in Science*, Cambridge University Press 1985.
5 The Association for Science Education *Alternatives for Science Education* (1979) and *Education Through Science* (1981).

6 J.F. Kerr *Practical Work in School Science*, Leicester University Press (Leicester) 1964. A partial replication of this work can be found in J.W. Beatty and B.E. Woolnough 'Practical work in 11–13 science: the context, type and aims of current practice' *British Educational Research Journal* Volume 8 (1982) pages 23–30.

7 C.G. Carré and J.O. Head *Through the Eyes of the Pupil*, McGraw-Hill (UK) (Maidenhead) 1974.

8 J.O. Head and M. Shayer 'Loevinger's ego development measures – a new research tool?' *British Educational Research Journal* Volume 6 (1980) pages 21–27.

9 J.S. Bruner *Towards a Theory of Instruction*, Norton (New York) 1968.

10 J.D. Novak 'An alternative to Piagetian psychology for science and mathematics education' *Studies in Science Education* Volume 5 (1978) pages 1–30.

11 D. Elkind *Children and Adolescents*, Oxford University Press (New York) 1970.

FURTHER READING

Bernstein, J. *Experiencing Science* Burnett/Andre Deutsch (London) 1979.
Contains thoughtful reappraisals of such figures as Kepler, Lysenko, Godel and Rosalind Franklin.
Chalmers, A.F. *What is This Thing Called Science?* Open University Press (Milton Keynes) 1978.
A straightforward introduction to the nature of science including a critique of inductivism and descriptions of the work of Popper and Kuhn.
Driver, R. *The Pupil as Scientist?* Open University Press (Milton Keynes) 1983.
Ros Driver was one of the first workers in Britain to advocate the constructivist perspective in science education and this book provides a clear account of that perspective.
Easlea, B. *Fathering the Unthinkable* Pluto Press (London) 1983.
In this book Easlea brings together two strands of his work: studies of the economics of the cold war and of conflict between the sexes, to sound a warning about the current international situation, in particular the role adopted by many male scientists.
Harding, J. *Switched Off: The Science Education of Girls* Longman/ Schools Council (London) 1983.
Jan Harding gives a clear, up-to-date review of the relevant research followed by a discussion of the possible implications and interventions.
Hudson, L. *Frames of Mind (Methuen) 1968.* (Also available in a Penguin edition).
The second, and generally better, book which Hudson wrote on this area. Many of his ideas have been challenged in the last decade but his books are very readable and rich with stimulating ideas.
Kelly, A. *The Missing Half: Girls and Science Education* Manchester University Press 1981.
A useful collection of essays by several authors, giving comprehensive coverage of this subject.

Maslow, A.H. *The Psychology of Science: A Reconnaissance* Harper and Row (New York) 1966.
More of a personal perspective than a reconnaissance, thin on evidence but offers interesting thoughts on the subject.

Medawar, P.B. *Induction and Intuition in Scientific Thought* Methuen (London) 1969.
This is only one of Medawar's readable books related to our concerns, although this one most directly attacks the central issue.

Polanyi, M. *Personal Knowledge* Routledge Kegan Paul (London) 1958.
An immensely influential book written by a formerly practising scientist who moved into philosophy. Not that easy to read, the arguments are close textured, but powerfully develop the thesis that knowledge, even within science, cannot be other than personal.

Rose, H. and Rose, S. *The Radicalisation of Science* Macmillan (London) 1976.
A challenging account of the extent to which science has become the tool of the few, to the loss of the many, in our society.

Roszac, T. *The Making of a Counter Culture* Faber (London) 1970.
The first book by the man who has emerged as a leading critic of the scientific culture within our society.

Shayer, M. and Adey, P. *Towards a Science of Science Teaching* Heinemann Educational Books (London) 1981.
The authors give an introduction to Piaget's ideas, a description of research carried out in the late 1970s within that tradition and discuss the implications for science education. The best introduction to the Piagetian perspective on science education.

Snow, C.P. *The Two Cultures: And a Second Look* Cambridge University Press 1965.
Still an interesting statement on this issue. Little has changed since the original Rede lecture in 1959.

Watson, J.D. *The Double Helix* Weidenfeld and Nicolson (London) 1968. (Also available in a Penguin edition).
Many of those involved in this saga were opposed to Watson publishing this account, and many others have been critical, particularly about his treatment of Rosalind Franklin. Nevertheless it remains a fascinating story, almost the only account of how scientists actually work and relate.

NAME INDEX

SUBJECT INDEX